"What a nice surprise to learn of your book, which brings some sanity to the outmoded economic model that is always on life support at the expense of someone else's life! You appear to have cracked the code of what actually is a functional economy – one that serves society rather than the other way around."

William R. Moomaw,
Professor Emeritus of International Environmental Policy,
Fletcher School of Law & Diplomacy,
Tufts University, and a lead author for the Intergovernmental Panel on
Climate Change (IPCC), which was awarded the 2007 Nobel Peace Prize.

"The Nordics stand out in international surveys in diverse ways: most democratic, happiest peoples, best for business, most prosperous and most livable cities. Jay Bragdon now adds another perspective: economic structures that mimic nature – an approach that allows both people, nature and economy to thrive. Reading the book from within the Nordics, it is an eye-opener. Although the Nordics still have a long way to go with regards to living in harmony with nature, Bragdon provides a vocabulary and an understanding that allow us to see what we are already doing right and therefore need to do even more."

Lene Rachel Andersen,
futurist, philosopher and author of
The Nordic Secret: A European Story of Beauty and Freedom.

"We live at an epochal time, where one economic worldview is dying and another is being born. Countries that lead this Copernican Revolution generate the world's highest living standards while lowering their ecological footprints. In keeping with the egalitarian, inclusive attributes of Nature, they are also rated as the world's healthiest and freest democracies. Jay Bragdon's important and timely research in this venue reveals the future that is emerging today. It is prescient and practical, a must-read for those exploring new possibilities for our economies, businesses and civilization."

Giles Hutchins,
author of *The Nature of Business* (2012),
The Illusion of Separation (2014) and *Future Fit* (2016),
and co-author of *Regenerative Leadership* (2019).

"Jay Bragdon is a consummate lifelong learner, systems thinker, model, and mentor for so many of us working with complex system change. His depth of understanding and the ability to expose the interconnectedness of the Nordic Model, old and new forms of capitalism, principles of sustainability, the power of culture and our ability to thrive in harmony with the natural world are beyond compare. Jay has the unique ability to articulate,

D1440940

translate and make accessible typically complex theories of change and financial models. This is an important read for anyone who cares about the urgency of addressing and achieving ecological, social and economic well-being for all, not just some. It is time for the ultimate paradigm shift!"

Darcy Winslow, co-founder and president,
Academy for Systems Change.

"An inspiring, hopeful, and superb book. Written with that rare combination of both common sense and striking data, the author unveils the 'Nordic secret' that's propelling what's rapidly emerging as the most robust, regenerative, and life-affirming form of capitalism in the world today. Jay Bragdon has nailed it. This business book is a must-read. It's a map—totally grounded in reality—for realizing a world of well-being, where business and economies can excel, all persons can thrive, and nature can flourish, now and across the generations."

David L. Cooperrider, PhD, distinguished university
professor and author of *Appreciative Inquiry: A Positive
Revolution in Change*; Char and Chuck Fowler Chair for
Business as an Agent of World Benefit, Case Western Reserve University

"Economies that mimic life is THE BIG IDEA at this critical moment in history. Mainstream economists, blinded by the neoclassical ideology of continuous GDP growth, miss the essential truth of this idea, which puts life at the center of economic decision-making; and society is now paying a deadly price in terms of ecological and financial overshoot. A contemporary proof of concept, the primary source of this transformative idea is a group of Nordic countries whose universal safety nets strengthen their free enterprise economies by investing them with healthy, educated and committed workforces. Jay Bragdon has revealed the essential truths of this system, which are as old as human culture itself."

John Fullerton, Founder of Capital Institute,
author of *Regenerative Capitalism* and
former Managing Director of JP Morgan.

"As one who has been born and raised in Sweden and now having many of my social projects in Sweden, it is interesting to consider the Nordic Model as life-mimicking. By framing our political-economic system as such, Jay Bragdon has discovered an implicit architecture underlying our prosperity that puts life ahead of GDP. This, of course, makes sense because people and Nature are the source of GDP. As a foundational ideal, however, it is precisely opposite the more common neoclassical model that puts GDP ahead of life – an industrial era mindset that has led to global climate change, social divisiveness and financial chaos. This is not to say our Nordic system is perfect. We still have a lot to learn. Nevertheless, as this book reveals, economies that mimic life offer an adaptable, believable pathway to the future that our over-stressed world so desperately needs."

Tomas Björkman, founder of the Ekskäret Foundation,
former chair of the EFG investment Bank
and author of *The World We Create* (2019).

For my friend Tom. With all best wishes, —Jay

ECONOMIES THAT MIMIC LIFE

The world economy today is at an historical inflection point. The neoclassical (industrial) model of economics is self-destructing while a new life-mimicking model, based on radically different assumptions, is emerging. Although rarely acknowledged in economic journals, Nordic countries, which pioneered the life-mimicking model, have become world leaders in prosperity and productivity while those operating on the older neoclassical/industrial model are trapped in downward spirals.

By approaching economies as sub-systems of life rather than super-systems that transcend life, we gain transformative insights. Such thinking led to the first circular economy experiments in Kalundborg (Denmark) during the 1970s, then quickly spread to the rest of the Nordic world. By placing a higher value on living assets (people and Nature) than on non-living capital assets, this approach generates harmony rather than exploitation and conflict. Because Nordic people feel vested in the system and responsible for its success, they are extraordinarily innovative and productive. That is why Nordic companies are regularly rated among the world's most sustainable and profitable in their fields – even though their region holds less than half of one percent of the world's population.

Written in an accessible way for non-economists, this book is ideal for readers interested in the benefits of biomimicry and methods of guiding democratic countries along a proven path of self-renewal. *Economies that Mimic Life* will also provide useful background for corporate leaders in scenario planning and strategic thinking. Knowing which way the political-economic wind is blowing will become increasingly important to corporate survival.

Joseph H. Bragdon is an investment advisor to high net worth families. *Economies that Mimic Life* is his third book on the general subject of biomimicry in business and economics. He is a pioneer in the field of corporate stewardship.

ECONOMIES THAT MIMIC LIFE

From Biomimicry to Sustainable Prosperity

Joseph H. Bragdon

Routledge
Taylor & Francis Group
LONDON AND NEW YORK

First published 2021
by Routledge
2 Park Square, Milton Park, Abingdon, Oxon OX14 4RN

and by Routledge
52 Vanderbilt Avenue, New York, NY 10017

Routledge is an imprint of the Taylor & Francis Group, an informa business

© 2021 Joseph H. Bragdon

The right of Joseph H. Bragdon to be identified as author of this work has been asserted by him in accordance with sections 77 and 78 of the Copyright, Designs and Patents Act 1988.

All rights reserved. No part of this book may be reprinted or reproduced or utilized in any form or by any electronic, mechanical, or other means, now known or hereafter invented, including photocopying and recording, or in any information storage or retrieval system, without permission in writing from the publishers.

Trademark notice: Product or corporate names may be trademarks or registered trademarks, and are used only for identification and explanation without intent to infringe.

British Library Cataloguing-in-Publication Data
A catalogue record for this book is available from the British Library

Library of Congress Cataloging-in-Publication Data
Names: Bragdon, Joseph H., 1939- author.
Title: Economies that mimic life: from bio-mimicry to sustainable prosperity / Joseph H. Bragdon.
Description: Abingdon, Oxon; New York, NY: Routledge, 2021. | Includes bibliographical references and index.
Identifiers: LCCN 2020040503 (print) | LCCN 2020040504 (ebook) | ISBN 9780367625979 (hbk) | ISBN 9780367625993 (pbk) | ISBN 9781003109877 (ebk)
Subjects: LCSH: Quality of life. | Sustainable development. | Economics.
Classification: LCC HN25.B73 2021 (print) | LCC HN25 (ebook) | DDC 304.2–dc23
LC record available at https://lccn.loc.gov/2020040503
LC ebook record available at https://lccn.loc.gov/2020040504

ISBN: 978-0-367-62597-9 (hbk)
ISBN: 978-0-367-62599-3 (pbk)
ISBN: 978-1-003-10987-7 (ebk)

Typeset in Joanna
by Deanta Global Publishing Services, Chennai, India

CONTENTS

DEDICATION AND ACKNOWLEDGMENTS

From start to finish, this book draws on the brilliant thinking of my late friend and colleague, Donella Meadows. As lead author of the 1972 classic, *Limits to Growth*, she and her MIT-based co-authors warned that growth-driven economic strategies were on a collision course with reality by rapidly depleting the very resources on which their strategies depended. Although widely criticized at the time as needlessly alarmist, today, nearly half a century later, their dire warnings seem prescient as the prevailing GDP-focused "neoclassical" approach to political-economy, self-destructs in a vortex of ecosystem degradation, climate change and runaway debt.

In spite of this unfolding tragedy, Dana (as she was known to friends) fervently believed humanity would come to its senses. She was fond of saying, "We have just enough time" to set the world economy on a new, more sustainable course if we put our collective minds to work on it. To accelerate that movement, she founded in 1996 the Sustainability Institute, a "think-do tank" devoted to imagining regenerative new ways forward. The "do" part of the Institute was a co-housing community and a working farm, where dedicated staff lived and worked together in a sustainable hillside village. Because of Dana's reputation as a visionary leader and mentor, many staff gave up promising academic and commercial careers to join her venture.

In 2000 Dana invited me, an investment advisor to high net worth families, and my wife (Jeanne), to serve on her board. At the time, I was researching a new model of business and economics centered on the primacy of living assets (people and Nature) compared to non-living capital assets – a reversal of traditional neoclassical/industrial thinking. Jeanne, a deep ecologist with a JD and LLM in environmental law and ethics, was my primary thinking partner. Together, we shared Dana's belief that transformative change was possible if a critical mass of visionary thinkers and doers showed the way forward. This book validates that belief.

One of Dana's most important insights concerned the power of leverage points: "places within a complex system (a corporation, an economy, a living body, a city, an ecosystem) where a small shift in one thing can produce big changes in everything."[1] That shift today is manifest in an emerging awareness that economies and companies are *sub-systems of life* rather than super-systems that are separate from and above life. Countries that initially shaped this mental model are now world prosperity leaders – advantages they have achieved on balanced budgets while also reducing their ecological footprints. Nowhere is this more evident than in the development of five Nordic economies (Denmark, Finland, Sweden, Norway, Iceland), a story we will follow throughout this book.

Sadly, the year after Jeanne and I joined the Sustainability Institute's board, Dana died, leaving her community bereft but determined to carry on in the spirit of advancing her vision, values and ideals. That is the spirit I bring to these pages. It is a joyful one, full of hope and promise for the future.

In addition to Dana, I would like to acknowledge some brilliant colleagues in the field of systems thinking who have profoundly influenced my work. Foremost among these is Peter Senge, whose book The Fifth Discipline, led me into the field of systems analysis. The Society for Organizational Learning (SoL), which he founded, published my first book, Profit For Life, which introduced the core elements of my life-mimicking model. In addition to Peter, I am greatly indebted to Darcy Winslow, co-founder and President of the Academy for Systems Change, and to others on its faculty and board (including Peter) whose questions and encouragement inspired me to look deeper into the world of political-economy from a systems perspective.

As my manuscript took shape, I was also fortunate to have advice from Lene Rachael Andersen, a Danish economist, futurist and lead author of *The Nordic Secret*. She and her book contributed greatly to my understanding of Nordic culture – especially how its shared holistic philosophy of education transformed the region from one of the poorest in Europe to one of the most prosperous in the space of three generations. Over the space of several months, Lene read through my manuscript twice, each time contributing valuable nuances that added important detail to my text.

Friends and colleagues in the field of regenerative business practices – particularly Giles Hutchins and Carolina Fernandez-Jansink – added important dimensions to my research on Nordic entrepreneurship and corporate management.

Above all, I am grateful to my wife, Jeanne, who had an important voice in creating this book. She read each chapter multiple times for content and flow with a goal of making them clear and accessible to a wide audience of readers. This is critically important to both of us because the more people know about the success of Nordic life-mimicking practices, the more likely they will be to advocate for systemic reform and a world hospitable to future generations of human and biospheric life.

Joseph H. (Jay) Bragdon

Note

1 Donella Meadows. 1999. "Leverage Points." The Sustainability Institute. http://don ellameadows.org/archives/leverage-points-places-to-intervene-in-a-system/

ECONOMIES THAT MIMIC LIFE – FROM BIOMIMICRY TO SUSTAINABLE PROSPERITY

Introduction

The world economy is presently at an historical inflection point. The neo-classical (industrial) model of economics is self-destructing, while a new life-mimicking model, based on radically different assumptions, is emerging. The new model is premised on an understanding that economies are sub-systems of life rather than super-systems that are separate from and above life. Consequently, they place a higher value on living *assets* (people and Nature) than on non-living capital assets – an ideal based on the reality that living assets are the source of capital assets and, indeed, all economic value. This reversal of traditional industrial doctrine is revolutionizing capitalism by attuning it to the living world that all economic systems ultimately depend upon.

Countries at the leading edge of this paradigm shift in political-economic thinking are today the *world's most effective market economies*. Meanwhile, countries adhering to the older mechanistic (industrial) model have become trapped in a negative cycle of ecosystem degradation, social stress and debt that is destroying the very foundations of their political-economies.

Table 0.1 Comparison of working assumptions and practices

	Living System Model	Traditional Model
Economies	Sub-systems of biosphere, society	The dominant system
Governance	Egalitarian, networked, decentralized	Hierarchical, centralized
Mission	Maintain healthy living systems	Maintain authority, control
Values	Primacy of living assets (people, Nature)	Primacy of non-living capital
Vision	Optimize living assets (circular economy)	Optimize GDP, profit
Leverage	Living asset stewardship (inspiration)	Financial gearing (debt)
Mind-set	Holistic, qualitative (non-linear)	Reductive, quantitative (linear)
Metrics	Focus on learning, adaptation (means)	Focus on results (ends)
Learning	Multiple loop (open-ended)	Single loop (follow the rules)
Risk	Being only generally right (Lack of precision, control)	Being precisely wrong (e.g., climate change)

The differences between these two models become starkly evident when we compare their underlying assumptions and practices. As shown in Table 0.1, these differences reveal a radical shift in worldview – much like the era when humanity realized the world was round rather than flat. By enabling people to imagine the world through a transformative new lens, such a shift in assumptions releases bursts of insight, knowledge and creativity that take human civilization to new levels of accomplishment.

Just as the round world insight released changes in navigation, exploration, science and trade that led to the modern era, the insight that economies are sub-systems of Nature has released a cascade of new technologies and methods that enable us to live more sustainably within the resources of our increasingly crowded and resource-stressed planet.

As we shall see in this book, countries on the leading edge of the living system model – particularly the Nordic five of Denmark, Finland, Sweden, Norway and Iceland – are consistently ranked at the top of global surveys on prosperity, productivity, quality of life, human development, social progress and happiness. They are also world leaders in financial stability based on their high gross domestic savings rates, low sovereign debt ratios and well-capitalized banking systems.

The key to the success of life-mimicking economies, as revealed in Table 0.1, is primarily cultural. While biology determines what we need, culture determines how we get it.

Importantly, the foregoing attributes of living systems are implicit in Nordic culture – an authenticity that gives them unique staying power. Whereas these qualities have roots in ancient Norse mythology and 16th-century Lutheran theology, they became a unified force during the mid-19th-century through a holistic philosophy of education that deepened people's sense of connection to Nature, the welfare of society and the security of future generations. Described in Chapter Three as "The Nordic Secret," this integrative philosophy was a forerunner to what we now call "systems thinking," and it endowed Nordic people with a sense of responsibility to serve the common good. Although other countries have adopted important elements of the life-mimicking model, this book will focus primarily on the Nordics because they have become the modern gold standard.

One of the most remarkable attributes of the holistic Nordic Model was its evolution in the midst of the Industrial Revolution — a time influenced by opposing beliefs that humans were masters and controllers of Nature. Before that era, when people lived closer to Nature, eco-centered value systems and philosophies were more common. Some of the best known ones emerged roughly 2,500 years ago — ranging from Thales, founder of the Milesian school of natural philosophy to Lao-Tse and Confucius in China and the Buddha in India. Later in history, the 11th-century neo-Confucian philosopher Zhang Zai wrote about the need for people (loosely translated) to "respect Heaven, love Nature, be compassionate to others and live your true self" — recognizing that the well-being of others and the well-being of oneself are two sides of the same coin.[1] In this context, important elements of the Nordic Model have long been embedded in human culture.

Affirmations of the life-mimicking model

As often happens at important historic turning points, the definitive qualities of new paradigms are not widely recognized until long after they evolved. Such is the case with the life-mimicking model. While this book is the first to formally describe this new paradigm, it is supported by a legacy of prior research and analysis in the fields of system dynamics, industrial ecology, biomimicry and human cognition.

The idea that traditional economic theory was failing, and that a new approach was needed, arose during the 1960s when world population growth and rapid industrialization had begun to outrun Earth's biological carrying capacities. This prompted a group of MIT researchers to do a computer simulation on the risks of status quo economics based on the emerging field of system dynamics. Their analysis, published in a 1972 report titled Limits to Growth, became an international wake-up call. Produced under the sponsorship of the Club of Rome, a global non-profit concerned with the future of humanity and the planet, it sold more than 30 million copies worldwide, igniting new fields of research in both economics and corporate management.[2]

Although identifying problems with the neoclassical model of economics was an important step, it took roughly four decades before a serious paper appeared on the idea that economies are sub-systems of anything. That changed, however, in 2015 when Herman Daly, a former senior economist at the World Bank, published an essay titled "Economics for a Full World" in which he stated that economies are "subsystems of the ecosphere."[3]

While Daly's thesis was long overdue, it was preceded in fact by the abovementioned five Nordic economies, which had already developed key elements of the life-mimicking model. This book is about their journey, which started in Kalundborg, Denmark, during the 1970s. To explain how it evolved and how it works at a granular level, our narrative will be enriched with stories illustrating the extraordinary economic results of this emerging new system.

As will be seen in the following nine chapters, the success of the Nordic Model emerges from the coherence of its eco-centric value system. Because of this, it predisposes people to think of economies as a means to serve life (broadly defined as people and Nature) rather than subordinating life in service to gross domestic product (GDP) growth. Since life is the primary source of all economic value, means and ends converge in the Nordic Model, rather than conflict as they do in the older industrial era model. This convergence generates a cascade of synergetic leverage points, as will be shown in Appendix One.

The wonderful thing about these leverage points is how they support open, collaborative organization structures energized by free-flowing information and open feedback – attributes that naturally generate innovative, life-serving behaviors and outcomes. By virtue of such self-reinforcing attributes, Nordic economies have gone from strength to strength, which is why Nordic people are regularly viewed as the world's happiest, healthiest and most prosperous.

By comparison, the older (neoclassical) model seeks leverage by borrowing from the theory that accelerating economic activity will more than pay for itself. The blind spot in this analysis, however, is that debt must be repaid. In situations where it grows faster than GDP for sustained periods, it actually harms economies, as shown in Appendix Four.

Because of such negative consequences, world debt has become one of the biggest problems facing industrial economies today. Currently growing at three or more times the rate of global GDP (depending on whether unfunded liabilities are included in the total), debt diverts incomes from supporting productive activities to paying down principal and interest.

In the US, for example, debt has grown so much faster than its economy that its true (debt-adjusted) per capita GDP is among the world's lowest according to a 2019 Bloomberg analysis.[4] This has seriously weakened the country and its middle class, whose prosperity and economic activity were once a source of strength and stability.

Exacerbating this problem is the neoclassical model's habitual reliance on fossil fuels — a depleting resource with increasingly adverse impacts on human and natural life. In addition to such harmful effects, the world's largest industrial countries today spend vast sums subsidizing fossil fuel companies and protecting global access to fossil fuel supplies via military spending — activities that deepen the debt trap into which their economies have fallen.

Rather than attending to the causes of these harmful conditions, neoclassical economists today make them worse by doubling down on failed policies, which typically call for more extensive use of fossil fuels, military spending and debt. This has created what physicist-historian Thomas Kuhn called "anomalies" — events that deviate from what is expected. Given the prevalence and severity of such anomalies today, they have become "systems traps" — disorders that exceed debt traps because they generate public distrust and hopelessness. In doing so, they dampen labor participation rates, increase public dependency and undermine the democratic freedoms that healthy economies require for healthy idea exchanges.

Because of the noted differences in culture and practices between the life-mimicking Nordic Model and the more conventional neoclassical model, Kuhn would say the two models are "incommensurable," which means one cannot be understood in terms of the other.

For this reason, well-intentioned efforts to merge the two cultures will not work because their models and fundamental values clash. Consequently, if countries wish to transition from the older industrial paradigm to the up-and-coming life-mimicking one, they must organize and manage the way Nordic countries do: by partnering with Nature; by investing in their citizens' health, education and welfare and by adopting egalitarian, democratic systems of governance – conditions that enable political-economies to adapt as world conditions change.

To those of us living in the US, it is hard to imagine that Nordic countries – four of which border on the Arctic Circle – now enjoy a better quality of life than we do. Much of the credit for this resides in the quality of Nordic universal safety nets, which endow their people with the skills and the will to sustainably amplify the region's economic resources. Although often described by US critics as "socialist," these safety nets in fact reinforce free market capitalism by raising the quality of human capital and by giving Nordic citizens the security to explore new ideas and innovate.

These generative feedbacks are affirmed by numerous success stories, including the high number of Nordic companies in annual listings of the esteemed "Global 100" (listed in Appendix Two); the stability of Nordic banks (eight of which were included among the world's 50 "safest banks" for 2019)[5] and the ubiquity of entrepreneurial events, such as the Nordic Cleantech Open, which deepen regional skills in sustainable economic development. Considering the region's small population (less than half of one percent of the world's population), short growing seasons and geographically dispersed markets, Nordic countries perform exceptionally well on these economic fronts.

Regional environmental policies, often coordinated by the Nordic Council of Ministers (NCM), incentivize the development of technologies in the fields of industrial ecology, bio-innovation, renewable energy and circular economy solutions by using a variety of economic instruments, including carbon taxes and public–private partnerships. Such policies, as we shall see, have demonstrably accelerated Nordic leadership in these global growth sectors.

The success of such initiatives, in turn, have generated important multiplier effects, including the development of advanced electronic networks (via digitalization and the Internet of Things) plus a robust community of entrepreneurial startups that feed off these emerging technologies. On the strength of these economic developments, Nordic governments generally balance their budgets. With few demands for official borrowing, capital is free to explore new opportunities.

Thanks to the quality of their human capital and eco-effective technologies, Nordic countries are normally in the top tier of global quality of life surveys. To outsiders who object to the region's high individual tax rates, Nordic citizens clearly feel they get their money's worth in return.

There are compelling reasons for paying attention to these small countries on the edge of Europe. The first is that they have reached the future first. They are grappling with problems that other countries too will have to deal with in due course, such as what to do when you reach the limits of big government. And the Nordics are coming up with highly innovative solutions that reject the tired orthodoxies of left and right.

The Economist, 2013[6]

Managing by means

The Nordic Model of attending to the health of the region's living assets is described in this book as managing by means (MBM) because people and Nature are the primary means of value creation.[7] When these critical assets are healthy, the system is healthy. And vice versa.

This qualitative approach is conceptually and pragmatically very different from the more traditional method of managing by results (MBR). By placing higher priorities on the quantities of GDP and profit produced, rather than the well-being of their primary assets (people and Nature), neoclassical economists create inherent conflicts between means and ends – a clash that ultimately subverts both GDP and profit. When countries fall into this systems trap, they are forced to borrow more and more in order to attain their GDP targets. That explains why the world's three largest economies (US, China, Japan) today have unsustainably high (and growing) debt-to-GDP ratios.

If we could pick one example of Nordic MBM practice that exemplifies the region's skills in partnering with Nature, it would be their approach to energy. Today two-thirds of Nordic electricity is generated from renewables (wind, biomass, solar, hydro, geothermal). Compared to electricity generated from fossil fuels, these sources have significantly higher energy returns on investment (EROIs). In addition, they confer important multiplier effects as they feed through regional economies. With such efficiency gains, Nordic people today are approaching what Norwegian scholars Nina Witoszek and Atle Midtun call "sustainable modernity."[8]

This is not to say Nordic economies are problem-free. In spite of making considerable progress in reducing their ecological footprints (including those in their supply chains), Nordic economies remain far from the true sustainability goal of zero impact, as revealed in Appendix Three. Understanding that they still have much to learn in their quest to live and work more sustainably, the Nordic Council of Ministers has created a system of "integrating environmental and economic accounts" that enables leaders and concerned citizens to learn and adapt as they strive to partner more harmoniously with life.[9] In the same spirit of reaching higher, the Prime Ministers' vision is to become "the most sustainable and integrated region in the world by 2030."

If humanity is to find a sustainable way forward, this is the path we must take. Because it is a path rather than a destination, the living system model is refreshingly open to learning from Nature and human error – qualities that endow it with virtually unlimited possibilities for adaptation and advancement. This, of course, requires humility and letting go of preconceived notions, particularly the industrial era beliefs, that we have a right to dominion over Nature by virtue of our intellect and scientific knowledge.

Importantly, the energy released by this ongoing quest for learning and insight awakens the human spirit, which is the source of our highest spiritual intelligence (SQ). Understanding the power of SQ, Steve Jobs redefined MBM as "management by meaning" – a reflection on the inspired learning that emerged from Apple Computer, the company he co-founded.

Because the life-mimicking (organic) model is so radically different from the neoclassical (industrial) model, and so often misconstrued by conventional political-economic leaders, it needs to be framed and described in a common-sense way that anyone can understand. That is the goal of this book. For readers who want a deeper, more detailed understanding of how it works, each chapter is supplemented by endnotes on sources of data and where to look for additional information.

The story of this emerging new paradigm is fascinating and rarely acknowledged in economic journals and texts. By drawing attention to its synergies, we begin to understand its inner strengths and why it is the most secure path to the future of life on Earth.

Notes

1 Guo, H and McDaniel, J. "The Western inscription: a gift from China to the world," *Open Horizons*. Available from: https://www.openhorizons.org/

the-western-inscription-a-gift-from-china-to-the-world.html   [Accessed June 29, 2020].

2 Meadows, D et al. 1972. *Limits to Growth*. Washington, DC: Potomac Associates – Universe Books.

3 Daly, H. 2015. "Economics for a full world," *Great Transition Initiative*. Available from: http://www.greattransition.org/publication/economics-for-a-full-world [Accessed June 29, 2020].

4 Del Giudice, V and Lu, W. 2019. "America's wealth hinges on its ability to borrow big – or else," *Bloomberg*. August 31. Available from: https://www.bloomberg.com/news/articles/2019-08-31/america-s-wealth-hinges-on-its-ability-to-borrow-big-or-else [Accessed June 29, 2020].

5 Sanders, D. 2019. "The world's safest banks 2019," *Global Finance Magazine*. November 8. Available from: https://www.gfmag.com/magazine/november-2019/worlds-safest-banks-2019 [Accessed June 29, 2020].

6 The Economist. 2013. "Northern lights," *The Economist*. February 2. p. 2. Available from: https://www.economist.com/sites/default/files/20130202_nordic_countries.pdf [Accessed June 29, 2020].

7 The term "Managing by Means" was first used by H Thomas Johnson and Anders Broms (2000) in a book they co-authored titled *Profit Beyond Measure*. (New York: The Free Press).

8 Witoszek, N and Midtun, A, eds. 2018. *Sustainable Modernity: The Nordic Model and Beyond*. Oxon: Routledge. Available from: https://www.amazon.com/Sustainable-Modernity-Routledge-Studies-Sustainability/dp/1138718211 [Accessed June 29, 2020].

9 Nordic Council of Ministers. 2016. *Making the Environment Count*. Available from: https://norden.diva-portal.org/smash/get/diva2:915431/FULLTEXT01.pdf [Accessed June 29, 2020].

1

THE SIX QUALITIES OF LIFE-MIMICKING CULTURES

The crises of our time ... are the necessary impetus for the revolution now under way. And once we understand nature's transformative powers, we see that it is our powerful ally, not a force to be feared or subdued.

Thomas S. Kuhn, 1962[1]

I offer nothing more than simple facts, plain arguments, and common sense.

Thomas Paine, 1776[2]

Economies that mimic life are showing the world a more robust form of free market capitalism. Centered on strengthening the primary means of value creation (people and Nature), they avoid the inner contradictions of neoclassical economic theory, where people and Nature are exploited and often degraded to generate profit and GDP.

The best exemplars of this emerging model are the Nordic countries of Denmark, Finland, Sweden, Norway and Iceland. By working in harmony with people and Nature, they have achieved remarkable productivity and prosperity, while countries trapped in the older industrial model struggle under mountains of debt and the accumulating costs of their social and ecological negligence.

The success stories of these exemplary Nordic nations are based on simple facts, plain arguments and common sense. With such reasoning, there is little need for the tortuous mathematical simulations of neoclassical economists, whose models increasingly serve the interests of those at the center of political-economic power rather than the wellbeing of the whole.

Framed as such, there is a striking similarity between Nordic visions of the future and those expressed by Thomas Paine in *Common Sense*. Writing on the eve of the American Revolution, Paine proclaimed, "We have it in our power to begin the world over again." By which he meant creating a new system of self-government free from the domineering constraints of centralized power.

Although the Nordic Model has been more evolutionary than revolutionary, drawing on centuries of humanistic and biophilic tradition, it became visibly activist in the 1970s when the world economy entered into ecological overstep. This, as we shall see, marked the beginning of the Nordic circular economy movement, which has since evolved into a renaissance of life-mimicking enterprise.

By elevating the importance of life in political-economic decision-making over the past half-century, Nordic economies have fundamentally shifted the terms of governance and market behavior. This philosophical shift naturally permeates differences in political-economic goal-setting. Whereas the primary aim of the neoclassical school is to optimize the *quantity of GDP and profit* — thus tacitly allowing economies to override people and Nature in pursuit of their goals — leaders in life-mimicking cultures aim to strengthen the *quality (resiliency) of life*. The wisdom of this life-centered approach, as mentioned in the Introduction, is its focus on the wellbeing of people and the planet, which are the primary sources (means) of all value creation.

These cultural and philosophical differences also play out in how institutions organize. To optimize idea sharing and collaboration, Nordic organizations generally replicate the decentralized, networked, open structures of living systems, where decision-making is localized (thus making them more responsive to their operating environments). Likewise, Nordic governments encourage citizen participation and feedback at all levels in order to make their political-economies more adaptable and effective.

By so engaging their citizens and voluntary civic organizations in thinking, planning and problem solving, Nordic organizations learn and adapt more quickly than those governed by more traditional hierarchical lines of authority, which assume that those at the top know best. Since the inception of ecological overstep in the early 1970s, such cultural differences have become increasingly important as Earth's biosphere becomes more fragile and dangerous to the health of all life, including our own.

Because the Nordic Model is more adept at learning and self-correcting than the traditional hierarchical model, countries in that region increasingly rate at the top of global surveys on prosperity, productivity, creativity, freedom of expression and happiness. Moreover, they do this with balanced budgets, high savings rates, secure social safety nets and low debt ratios – qualities that have made them world leaders in political-economic stability and progress.

So how do we define economies that mimic life? As shown in Table 1.1, there are six generic qualities that support both life and economic progress. This chapter will briefly review all six and review how they benefit humanity and the biosphere. Subsequent chapters will explore in more detail how these qualities have made Nordic economies the world leaders they are today.

Table 1.1 Attributes of economies that mimic life

Life-Mimicking Attributes	Economic Effects
Unified, decentralized, networked organization (like a living cell).	Cohesive social capital networks amplify communication and effectiveness.
While the Federal Reserve approach to learning that replicates the self-regenerating processes of Nature.	People feel empowered, engaged, eager to learn, innovate and contribute.
Frugal instincts and behavior that respect Earth and its resources.	Conserves energy and natural resources, reduces costs, increases efficiency.
Openness to feedback from all sources as ecosystem conditions change.	Catalyzes speed of learning, adaptation and ability to function sustainably.
Symbiotic vision and sense of purpose serves the health of all.	Strengthens co-operation and collaboration among economic players within the system.
Broad spectrum consciousness, sense of being within the whole system.	Develops strategic insight, sense of systemic limits and capacity for long-term planning.

These six attributes, which are common to all living systems, have an evolutionary history of roughly 4 billion years dating back to when life began on Earth. Even consciousness, which enables people to make complex, long-term choices, was present in early single cells as revealed by their ability to adapt, reproduce and nourish themselves.

If the foregoing six attributes seem unfamiliar as a descriptive framework for economics, that is because neoclassical (mainstream) economists tend to frame their theories in mechanistic terms – a practice that evolved during the industrial revolution. Nowhere is this more evident than in the use of credit, which most economists see as a lever to boost economic growth.

Perhaps blinded by the Archimedes Principle that the power of a lever increases with its size, mainstream economists have long encouraged nations, companies and consumers to borrow aggressively and take risks – even when the growth of borrowing exceeds the debt-carrying capacities of national incomes and GDP.

The fallacy of this mindset was powerfully exposed in the early stages of the 2020 global coronavirus pandemic when countries were forced to borrow massive sums to protect public health and to stabilize their economies. While those adhering to the life-mimicking model were able to manage by virtue of their low debt levels and productivity, those operating under the neoclassical model were forced into extreme hardship because their debt-carrying capacities were severely impaired. To fund the US Treasury's multi-trillion-dollar emergency borrowings, for example, the US Federal Reserve had to rapidly expand the money supply and drive interest rates to their lowest level on record. Nevertheless, in spite of such massive intervention, US credit markets collapsed into chaos. While the Federal Reserve blamed that collapse on the coronavirus, it was simply the pin that burst the massive US debt bubble that had been growing since the 1980s.

> From the late 1980s, central banks — and especially the Fed — conducted what came to be known as "asymmetric monetary policy", whereby they supported markets when they plunged but failed to damp them down when they were prone to bubbles. Excessive risk taking in banking was the natural consequence.
>
> John Plender, Financial Times, 2020[3]

To illustrate the scale of the US debt problem, its total credit market debt at the time of the coronavirus outbreak was $73.4 trillion (roughly 3.5 times GDP). When unfunded government liabilities (implicit debt) were added to this, its total arrears more than doubled.[4] Although this is an extreme example, most industrial economies were caught in a similar bind – one where a presumed leverage point (debt) became a debilitating systems trap and a burden when additional borrowing capacity was most needed.

Rather than seeking leverage through risk-taking and borrowing, Nordic countries pursue it by investing in the health, education and welfare of their citizens and by safeguarding natural resources. In so doing, they implicitly acknowledge that people and Nature are the primary sources of economic added value. Because of the synergies in this approach, they enjoy some of the world's highest standards of living (and lowest sovereign debt ratios), as will be revealed in subsequent chapters.

The simple wisdom of this approach resides in the fact that the health of an economy ultimately depends on the health of the whole system in which it exists. Like the human body, economies cannot function well if their critical parts are impaired. Consequently, when countries nurture people and Nature, they strengthen the whole, yielding a cascade of mutually-reinforcing returns to society and the biospheric web of life in which they exist.

As we look deeper into the life-mimicking Nordic Model in subsequent chapters, and the extraordinary operating leverage in its methods, we will see more clearly why Nordic countries are so prosperous and dynamic. In Chapters Two through Seven, for example, we explore each of the six attributes of life outlined in Table 1.1, showing how they contribute to regional prosperity, supported by definitive economic data, global survey results and examples of progressive Nordic business practices. Building on these insights, Chapter Eight considers the Nordic Model as an organic whole – in particular how it launched game-changing innovations in renewable energy and circular economy technologies that continually strengthen the model from within. Summing up, Chapter Nine ponders what we can learn from the Nordic Model by returning to the ethical ideals of Adam Smith, widely considered to be "the father of economics," and how his values in fact support life-mimicking cultures. Finally, in the Epilogue we see how these uplifting pragmatic ideals have enabled Iceland, a small country on the edge of the Arctic Circle, to generate a higher living standard than the US, based on the quality of its democracy and the extraordinary productivity of its citizens.

In telling these stories, we reveal through simple, verifiable facts how Nordic countries have achieved the world's highest standards by reversing the priorities of the neoclassical model. By attending first and foremost to the health and wellbeing of their primary assets (people and Nature) and by mimicking Nature's circular (renewable) processes, they are today showing the world a new sustainable path forward.

If we take a big step back from all competing theories of political economy, it is worth asking: "Is this not the result that most people want?"

Bringing clarity to a confused profession

As anyone who reads the business news knows, the economics profession is rife with different, often conflicting schools of thought. For a discipline that seeks the stature of science, economists display a perplexing lack of consensus plus a poor record of forecasting. That is because their profession is a discipline, not a science like physics. While physics can send satellites far into space and tell us when they will arrive at their destinations with remarkable precision, economists cannot even agree on the causes of the last global recession.

As neoclassical economists try to justify their abstract theories, they present us with so many disagreements on cause-and-effect that we end up with more confusion than clarity. To further complicate matters, the mathematical "proofs" they use to validate their opinions are beyond comprehension to the general public and most politicians, which makes it nearly impossible for ordinary people to understand or question their underlying assumptions. That deficiency, of course, blocks learning and generates distrust – neither of which advances human and biospheric wellbeing.

By recognizing the living world as it is, rather than one defined by neoclassical economic abstractions, we gain clarity. As Adam Smith famously said, "What improves the circumstances of the greater part can never be regarded as an inconvenience to the whole." Once people understand this bit of common sense, they tend to make better political and economic choices.

In keeping with Smith's observations, there appear to be strong correlations between the qualities of egalitarian democracies, where people can freely express their opinions, and the growth of economic prosperity. Worldwide, countries that share these qualities tend to rank in the top decile of global surveys on productivity, innovation, environmental health, social progress and quality of life. Significantly, Nordic countries have held leadership positions in all such surveys over multiple years.

Consider, for example, the annual democracy survey of 167 countries by the Economist Intelligence Unit (EIU). Based on five categories of democratic strength – *electoral process and pluralism; civil liberties; the functioning of government; political participation and political culture* – Nordic countries are virtually always rated in the top ten. In the 2019 survey, Norway was rated first as the most open democratic culture, followed by Iceland (second), Sweden (third), New Zealand (fourth), Denmark (fifth), Canada (sixth), Ireland (seventh), Finland (eighth), Australia (ninth) and Switzerland (tenth). The USA, by comparison, was rated 25th (a "flawed democracy") having been marked down from 23rd in 2017.[5]

Congruent with the EIU's Democracy Index, Transparency International gives Nordic countries top rankings in its 2019 Corruption Perceptions Index, which rates 180 nations on the trustworthiness of their cultures. Here again, we find Nordic countries in the elite top decile with Denmark and New Zealand (tied for first), Finland (third), Sweden, Switzerland and Singapore (tied for fourth), Norway (seventh), Netherlands (eighth), Germany and Luxembourg (tied for ninth), and Iceland (eleventh). The US, by comparison, dropped from 16th in 2017 to 23rd in 2018 due to "threats to its system of checks and balances as well as an erosion of ethical norms at the highest levels of power."[6]

The 2019 World Press Freedom Index, compiled annually by Reporters Without Borders, is an allied indicator that reveals the strength of democracy and public trust by evaluating freedom of information. Out of 180 countries surveyed, Nordic countries were again in the lead with Norway (first), Finland (second), Sweden (third), Netherlands (fourth) and Denmark (fifth) rated in the top five and Iceland (14th) rated in the top decile. In this survey, the USA dropped to 48th, a significant downgrade from its 2016 standing (43rd) – due primarily to the Trump Administration's attempts to discredit the news media and erode First Amendment rights on freedom of the press.[7]

We find similar results in the 2019 Freedom in the World Index compiled by Freedom House. Presented as an annual global report on political rights and civil liberties in 195 countries and territories, it is a barometer of liberal democratic norms that have long supported economic prosperity. Here too, we find Nordic countries clustered at the top with Finland rated first, Norway second, Sweden third, Canada fourth, Netherlands fifth, Australia sixth, New Zealand seventh, Uruguay eighth, Denmark ninth and Ireland tenth. Iceland was not rated in this survey, probably due to its small population. The US was rated 33rd, far behind the leaders.[8]

What we see in these surveys is a cultural pattern. While other countries rank close to the Nordics on the foregoing surveys, the Nordic five have become the gold standard of openness, transparency and democratic freedoms – qualities that enable them to learn and adapt as the living world about them changes. In this context, they operate much like an ecosystem, where each part of the system synergistically supports the health of the whole and vice versa.

The big picture that emerges from this data is how these inclusive, egalitarian (life-mimicking) qualities are more conducive to economic wellbeing and progress than hierarchical, GDP-focused (neoclassical) strategies ever could be. That is why these small countries on the northern frontier of Europe consistently lead the world in economic progress and quality of life – the very things economists should aim to cultivate.

> Many things of value in life cannot be fully captured by GDP, but they can be measured by metrics of health, education, political freedom, and the like.
>
> Justin Fox, Harvard Business Review, 2020[9]

Kalundborg: Where it all began

Kalundborg, Denmark – the site of the world's first industrial symbiosis – is a wonderful example of how the Nordic system works. As one of the world's most productive industrial centers, its culture brilliantly models the six life-mimicking qualities described in Table 1.1. Given its influence among its Nordic neighbors and other countries that aspire to the circular economy model, it can rightly be considered the godparent of economies that mimic life.

Kalundborg's story is particularly relevant because it transformed itself from an economy once dominated by fossil fuels (a coal-burning power plant and an oil refinery) into a global citadel of renewable energy, biotechnology and closed-loop manufacturing. With a population of only 16,500, the municipality is today an international symbol of how people with shared synergetic visions can infuse new life into economies operating under the older industrial capitalist model.

The transformation process began when municipal and business leaders started a series of experiments in resource sharing and recycling in the 1970s, fed by open exchanges of ideas and a shared vision of the common good. Guided by an awakening that the industrial world was pushing beyond its ecological limits – advanced by the renowned Norwegian ecologist Arne Naess – the citizens of Kalundborg created a symbiotic model where local wastes and industrial byproducts were transformed into value-added resources the same way Nature recycles and reuses spent nutrients.

As success led to success, Kalundborg became a global innovation hotspot and an important learning center. Today its exchange network comprises more than 30 bilateral or trilateral commercial agreements centered on exchanges of energy plus the recycling of water and waste products, all of which are overseen and coordinated by an adjacent symbiosis institute.

The tangible economic benefits of this symbiosis can be seen in the value generated by its four original leadership companies: Ørsted (the utility owner), which is now the world leader in offshore wind energy; Equinor (the refinery owner), a diversified energy company and world leader in carbon sequestration; Novo Nordisk, one of the world's most innovative and profitable pharmaceutical companies; and Novozymes, the world leader in enzyme technology. Often working in collaboration, these four have pioneered new circular economy solutions that have spread throughout the Nordic region.

In one such pioneering venture, Inbicon (a subsidiary of Ørsted) converted 30,000 metric tons per year of waste wheat straw supplied by local farmers into biofuels. Using waste steam from Ørsted's power station mixed with enzymes from Novozymes, it produced on an annual basis 5.4 million liters of bio-ethanol for the Equinor refinery; 13,100 tons of lignin pellets for use as boiler fuel at the power station and 11,200 metric tons of molasses for use as a livestock feed supplement plus bionutrients that can be returned to farmers as fertilizer. Based on this success, Inbicon now licenses its technology worldwide. By 2022 it envisions up to 500 commercial-scale biomass refineries in the US and Canada, producing 10 billion gallons of bio-ethanol a year and generating as much as 20,000 MW of green power.

As such creative innovations progressed, demand for Kalundborg's circular economy know-how quickly spread. Today the Symbiosis Center Denmark (Dansk Symbiosecenter) collaborates with universities, non-profits and other industrial symbioses, both in the Nordic region and worldwide. In addition, its BIOPRO development center – a partnership between Novo Nordisk, Novozymes, the Danish Technical University, the University of Copenhagen and nearby biotech companies – has become a leading research and learning center in the futuristic field of bio-innovation. Building on BIOPRO's success and growth potential, the Nordic Council of Ministers created in 2015 a Nordic bioeconomy panel, which subsequently made bio-innovation a central goal of future Nordic development.

The Novo Nordisk Foundation, which owns controlling interests in both Novo Nordisk and Novozymes, is also a major catalyst in the field of bio-innovation – both locally and worldwide. In addition to funding BIOPRO, the foundation supports a new center for biosustainability at the Technical University of Denmark (DTU), which researches and develops "cell factories" that produce organic substitutes for petrochemicals. Since these chemicals exist in countless everyday products, including those that people ingest (pharmaceuticals) or put on their skin (soap, cosmetics, textiles), such safe, bio-based chemicals have become one of the fastest-growing segments of the global chemistry industry.

> The market for Bio-based chemical is anticipated to grow from $6,474 million in 2016 to $23,976 million by 2025, at a CAGR of 16.16% between 2017 and 2025... [C]oncerns regarding the environment due to dangerous chemicals and depletion of fossil fuels are leading to the rise of the production of the bio-based chemicals.
>
> Bio-based News, 2017[10]

The remarkable thing about these developments and Kalundborg's evolution as a global leader in circular economy enterprise is that they developed organically at the local level based on the curiosity and collaboration of free-thinking citizens and companies committed to the health of the whole. Like symbiotic collaborations in Nature, these are rooted in mutual benefit – a quality that has stabilized and energized Kalundborg's economy as new needs and opportunities arise.

As discussed in Chapter Three, these holistic tendencies are supported by a philosophy of education and self-development that has been part of the Nordic cultural DNA since the middle of the 19th century. By urging people to think beyond themselves to the wider contexts of Nature, the wellbeing of society and the security of future generations, this philosophy endows Nordic people with an almost reflexive capacity for systems thinking.

Looking back on the transformation of Kalundborg from an industrial fossil-fuel-based economy to the symbiotic life-mimicking one it is today – all in the space of two generations – we find striking parallels with the earlier 14th-century European Renaissance that began in Florence.

By challenging established norms in fundamental ways, both movements can be seen as transformative historic events – ones that take us to new levels of understanding about our relationships with Nature, authority and ourselves.

The emerging Nordic Renaissance

The common element in both the European Renaissance and today's emerging Nordic Renaissance is an awakening to the narrow self-interests and corruption of centralized hierarchies. In 14th-century Europe, political and economic power was centralized in the Roman Catholic Church, feudal kings and their vassals who controlled virtually all wealth. Due to the extreme inequities of this system, most people lived in dire poverty and filth. One consequence of this was the proliferation of ectoparasites (human body lice and fleas) – a health hazard that eventually killed roughly a third of Europe's population with the Black Plague. Another consequence was the Hundred Years' War (1337–1453) that plunged the Plantagenet and Valois rulers of England and France deep into debt as they sought to leverage their power; a third consequence was the emergence of scientific insight, which called into question the authority of Church doctrine and opened possibilities that people could become masters of their own destinies.

Today's hierarchies, which also control most of the world's wealth, are primarily corporate. While companies have indeed succeeded in raising living standards, they have also become more feudal as their corporate power and political influence have congealed toward oligarchy – thus increasing disparities between rich and poor. In addition, national and corporate competition for resources have caused catastrophic damage to the biosphere, which now threatens all life on Earth. Like the excesses of 14th-century feudal authorities, those in power today seem inured to the damages they have created and dismiss scientific challenges to their authority as fake news or propaganda.

Just as the plague catalyzed the European Renaissance, the ten-fold increase in the price of oil during the 1970s catalyzed the Nordic one that began in Kalundborg. Because the economies of Denmark and its Nordic neighbors were small and relied heavily on imported oil, that sudden price increase became an existential threat. Compounding Danish concerns were two global recessions, the first of which (1973–1975) put an end to the post-World-War-II economic expansion, and the second (early 1980s), which led to high and rising European unemployment rates into 1985.

For Kalundborg, these wake-up calls prompted some of their earliest experiments in recycling and resource reclamation. As the success of these ventures grew through the 1980s and 1990s, they eventually took on a life of their own, giving rise to the Symbiosis Center Denmark (1996) and eventually the development of the Nordic region's life-mimicking circular economy model.

Looking back on the global economic shocks of that period, including the ongoing depletion of Earth's resources, it is remarkable how little change occurred in neoclassical economic thinking and industrial capitalist orthodoxy. Rather than finding ways to reduce resource consumption, as the citizens of Kalundborg did, the US government approached these challenges as ones that could be solved by exerting political, financial and military power. Its solution was the global "petrodollar system" whereby oil, the world's most actively traded commodity, would be priced in US dollars in exchange for US military protection. This arrangement, first struck with Saudi Arabia in 1973, was later extended to all OPEC countries (Organization of Petroleum Exporting Countries) in 1975. This, of course, created an immediate demand for dollars, solidifying its role as the world's key currency for purposes of trade.

Rather than being a durable solution, this gambit ultimately became a systems trap. Because the world's supply of dollars grew in sync with world trade, the US government and consumers were suddenly provided with a global pool of dollars from which they could borrow (and consume) more freely. To political-economic leaders motivated by GDP-first models, this seemed a dream come true. What they failed to recognize, however, was: (1) how it incentivized reckless borrowing to the point where debt started growing at a faster rate than GDP (as shown in Appendix Four) and (2) how the resulting surge in consumption accelerated the world economy's decline into ecological overshoot while oil solidified its role as the world's master industrial resource.

> Today humanity uses the equivalent of 1.75 Earths to provide the resources we use and absorb our waste.
>
> The Global Footprint Network, 2020[11]

As such realities closed in on the neoclassical GDP-first model, those near the center of power fiercely defended their authority — just as feudal hierarchies did during the late Middle Ages. We see this today in disturbing global trends toward oligarchy and "financialization" (trying to solve fundamental social and ecological problems via contrived financial interventions). We also see it in the rise of military spending as countries seek access to strategic resources (especially fossil fuels) and important global trade routes, all of which feed social discord and takes us deeper into ecological overshoot.

Taking note of this fraught situation, some political economists advocate for a middle path between the decaying neoclassical model and the emerging life-mimicking one. Reasonable as this sounds, however, it is impossible for two critical reasons: first, the two systems are incommensurable because they operate on radically different premises (as outlined in the Introduction), second, humanity's ecological overstep has gone so far that it can only be stopped by reversing course.

This does not mean destroying capitalism as defenders of the status quo proclaim nor does it portend a descent into the radical socialism of state-run economies. On the contrary, the life-mimicking Nordic Model is today the world's most robust form of capitalism. By recognizing that living assets (people and Nature) are the primary means of value creation, it strengthens economies and their capacities to generate value. The effectiveness of such management by means (MBM) practices are affirmed over and over by global surveys plus hard data on Nordic productivity and financial stability as we shall see. These are simple facts, grounded in plain argument and common sense.

To see how it works, read on.

Notes

1 Thomas Kuhn. 1962. *The Structure of Scientific Revolutions*. Chicago, IL: University of Chicago Press.
2 Thomas Paine. 1776. *Common Sense*. Philadelphia, PA: R. Bell.
3 J Plender. 2020. "The seeds of the next debt crisis," *Financial Times*. March 4. Available from: https://www.ft.com/content/27cf0690-5c9d-11ea-b0ab-339c2307bcd4 [Accessed June 29, 2020].
4 The amount of federal, state and local unfunded liabilities depends on a variety of actuarial assumptions, so they vary widely. According to the usdebtclock.org, unfunded liabilities at the end of fiscal year 2019 were more than double explicit credit market debt, suggesting the total US debt burden is three or more times larger than reported.
5 Current Affairs Today. 2019. "Democracy index 2019: key facts," *Current Affairs Today*. January 10. Available from: https://currentaffairs.gktoday.com/democracy-index-2019-key-facts-01201964364.html [Accessed January 3, 2020].
6 Corruption Perceptions Index 2019. https://www.transparency.org/en/cpi/2019#.
7 Reporters Without Borders. World Press Freedom Index 2019. https://rsf.org/en/2019-world-press-freedom-index-cycle-fear [Accessed June 29, 2020].
8 Freedom House. 2019. "Freedom in the world," *Freedom House*. Available from: https://freedomhouse.org/sites/default/files/Feb2019_FH_FITW_2019_Report_ForWeb-compressed.pdf [Accessed June 29, 2020].
9 Justin Fox. 2012. "The economics of wellbeing," *Harvard Business Review*. January-February 2012. Available from: https://hbr.org/2012/01/the-economics-of-well-being [Accessed June 29, 2020].
10 Bio-based News. 2017. "Global bio-based chemicals market forecast," *Bio-based News*. August 4. Available from: http://news.bio-based.eu/global-bio-based-chemicals-market-forecast-2017-2025/ [Accessed June 29, 2020].
11 Global Footprint Network. 2020. "Ecological footprint," *Global Footprint Network*. Available from: https://www.footprintnetwork.org/our-work/ecological-footprint/ [Accessed June 29, 2020].

2

THE VALUE OF SOCIAL CAPITAL NETWORKS

Social capital ... refers to features of social organization, such as trust, norms, and networks, that can improve the efficiency of society by facilitating coordinated actions.

Robert Putnam, 1993[1]

Countries must invest in social progress, not just economic institutions, to create the proper foundation for economic growth.

Michael Porter, 2015[2]

Economies are social capital networks organized to generate value and security for the people they serve. Those that operate most effectively, like the Nordic five, have cohesive democratic cultures where governments invest in the health, education and security of their citizens and where they ensure fundamental freedoms of speech, association and property ownership.

As noted in Chapter One, all five Nordic countries are rated at or near the top in global surveys on the integrity of their democracies, the honesty and transparency of their governments and the freedom of their media. As will be discussed in this chapter, they are also rated at the top in global surveys on economic progress, general prosperity, environmental health, personal happiness, productivity, mutual trust and other indicators of systemic health. Collectively, these attributes of social capital and competitive strength powerfully contribute to the region's advanced economic development and social stability.

The term "social capital" emerged from a 1993 book by Harvard professor Robert D. Putnam, titled *Making Democracy Work*. Although not directly focused on economics, his work nevertheless applies to many of the building blocks of strong economies – especially the synergetic effects of trust, reciprocity, information sharing and co-operation.

Quickly seeing these links, Francis Fukuyama brought Putnam's work into the domain of economics with his 1995 book, *Trust: The Social Virtues and the Creation of Prosperity*.[3] Two years later, a paper by Stephen Knack and Philip Keefer published in the *Quarterly Journal of Economics* titled "Does Social Capital Have an Economic Payoff?" took the idea more deeply into the field.[4] Looking back on this time, Sjoerd Beugelsdijk, writing in the *Oxford Economic Papers* (2004), declared the value of trust was "probably one of the most successfully introduced 'new' concepts in economics in the last decade."[5]

One of the most widely cited new papers on the subject, titled "Social Trust and Economic Growth," was written by Christian Bjørnskov, an economics professor at Aarhus University in Denmark. Written in January 2017 and later published in the *Oxford Handbook of Social and Political Trust*, it provided compelling evidence of the positive links between trust and economic results by showing strong statistical correlations between social trust and real per capita gross domestic product (GDP) plus industrial output. Significantly, Bjørnskov found the strongest correlations were in countries that had been "stably democratic for the past 20 years" – a result that robustly supports the economic advantages of the socially responsible, life-mimicking Nordic Model.[6]

To clarify these links, Bjørnskov noted that countries with high levels of social trust enjoy diverse economic benefits, including:

- Simplified investment decision-making, enabling individuals and institutions to "invest in riskier, but potentially more productive processes";

- Reduced transaction costs because trustworthy people are more likely to abide by formal rules and informal social contracts;
- Less need for government regulation and oversight;
- Diminished vigilance against theft, criminality and predatory litigation, which allows reallocating resources from protection to actual production;
- Reduced need for corporate bureaucracies to monitor and supervise employees, which feeds back to higher levels of employee morale and productivity;
- Improved flow of information and ideas through social and corporate networks, thereby boosting knowledge resources and innovation;
- Greater tolerance for ideas that challenge conventional wisdom, which continually refresh economic thinking.

Bjørnskov's findings have since been supported by two authoritative global databases: (1) the global Social Progress Index, a complementary metric to the more traditionally reported GDP, that was designed by professors Michael Porter from the Harvard Business School and Scott Stern from MIT's Sloan School of Management and (2) the Legatum Prosperity Index, compiled by the UK non-profit Legatum Institute.

The Social Progress Index measures what matters to citizens – health care, infrastructure and civil liberties – characteristics that are the very foundation of sustainable societies. Compiled in partnership with Deloitte, an accountancy, the index is based on 54 indicators of "basic human needs, foundations of well-being, and opportunity to progress." Since being launched in 2014, Nordic countries have consistently ranked in or near the top ten of the nations surveyed. In the latest 2019 survey, which covered 146 countries, Norway was rated first, Denmark second, Switzerland third, Finland fourth, Sweden fifth and Iceland sixth. By comparison, the US was rated 26th, a significant drop from its 2017 rank (18th).[7]

The 2019 Legatum Prosperity Index, based on surveys of 150 countries, came up with roughly similar results based on nine conditions required for prosperity, including: "Economic Quality, Business Environment, Governance, Personal Freedom, Social Capital, Safety and Security, Education, Health, and the Natural Environment." Here again, all five Nordic countries were in the top ten with Denmark (first), Norway (second), Sweden (fourth), Finland (fifth) and Iceland (tenth). The US, by comparison, was rated 18th.[8]

> Since the middle of the last century, the Nordic countries (Norway, Sweden, Finland, Denmark and Iceland) have been regarded as model social democracies ... Their citizens enjoy some of the highest living standards the world can offer, with an economic model that offers minimal barriers to free trade, fosters private ownership and promotes socially egalitarian outcomes, in conjunction with a generous welfare state.
>
> The Legatum Prosperity Index, 2018[9]

As will be shown later, the findings of these two indices are corroborated in numerous global surveys and supported by hard economic data. To understand why, it is important to first understand the foundations of social capital so we can see more clearly the relationships between these indicators and the beneficial economic outcomes they generate.

Foundations of Nordic social capital

Broadly speaking, there are three important elements of Nordic social capital. The first, and most widely recognized, is the strong universal safety net provided by their governments. These provide, at a minimum, free education and health care plus generous guaranteed pension plans for retirees. For citizens who are laid off or leave their jobs to pursue other opportunities, Nordic countries also offer "flexicurity" to help them feed their families and train for new jobs. Considered as a whole, these benefits free Nordic people to upgrade their skills and seek more fulfilling work without fear of failure or sinking into poverty. They also give citizens a sense of freedom to question policies and procedures that are not working and to offer innovative ideas – opportunities that often elude people who work in more traditional (hierarchical) venues.

The second element of Nordic social capital is their openness and transparency – cultural attributes that are reinforced by low levels of patronage and corruption. Together, these qualities bolster trust and collaboration, making it easier to do business without the delays and expense of executing lengthy background checks and contracts. It also makes citizens more inclined to respect government decisions and regulations and to willingly pay their fair share of taxes.

The third element is the cohesiveness of Nordic cultures, which strengthens regional co-operation on matters of common interest. As a community of independent states with similar historical, social, economic, cultural and political backgrounds, there is a "low psychic distance" between Nordic people – a foundation on which deeper integration can be based. This strong sense of identity combined with the region's deep-rooted life-affirming values makes it easier to share decisions and create regional projects, which are frequently done under the aegis of the Nordic Council of Ministers.

This strong sense of community interest and involvement is affirmed by a 2013 study by the Bertelsmann Stiftung Foundation titled "Measuring Common Ground – an International Comparison of Social Cohesion." Based on a detailed analysis of social networks, solidarity, participation, trust, fairness, respect for rules and civic participation over a period of nearly 25 years (1989 through 2012), the study concluded that Denmark, Norway, Sweden and Finland have the world's highest levels of social cohesion with a pronounced focus on "the common good" as measured by "prosperity, equitable income distribution and technological progress toward achieving a knowledge society."[10] Although Iceland was not included in this analysis, it is a charter member of the Nordic Council of Ministers, which often speaks for the larger group.

The strength of Nordic social cohesion is likewise validated by global surveys on the quality of countries' social safety nets, the openness and transparency of their governments, the freedoms enjoyed by their citizens and the press, the quality of their natural environments and the happiness of citizens. Given the similarities of Nordic rankings in these surveys, we find strong evidence of a shared culture that enables collaborative thinking and problem solving.

It is interesting to note, for example, how well Nordic social safety nets provide for retirement security – an area where the US government alone is underfunded by more than $50 trillion.[11] Instead of deferring such costs as many governments do, benefits are fully funded as earned.

According to a 2019 Global Retirement Index (GRI) by the French Investment company Natixis Global Asset Management, which covered

18 variables over four sub-categories – finances in retirement, material well-being, health, and quality of life – Nordic countries were solidly in the global top tier with Iceland rated first, Norway third, Sweden sixth, Demark seventh and Finland 12th. In the survey's important quality of life sub-index, Denmark was rated first, followed by Finland second, Norway fourth, Sweden sixth and Iceland eighth.[12]

Reflecting the Nordic community's trust in the stability and fairness of their social safety nets, they have also earned top ratings in the Fragile States Index. Published since 2005 by the US Fund for Peace and *Foreign Policy* magazine, index ratings are based on 12 key political, social and economic indicators and over 100 sub-indicators that provide "political risk assessment and early warning of possible conflicts" by highlighting "vulnerabilities that contribute to state fragility." Out of 178 nations surveyed in 2019, Nordic countries were all rated in the top ten with Finland first, Norway second, Denmark fourth, Iceland sixth and Sweden seventh. The US, whose rating has dropped significantly over the past five years, was rated 26th due to "significant political upheaval."[13]

The social capital of Nordic countries is further strengthened by their care for life in all its forms and their vigilance in safeguarding human health. This is validated by Yale University's 2018 Environmental Performance Index (EPI), which rated 180 countries on 24 indicators covering environmental health and ecosystem vitality. On the indicator that most closely correlates with citizen health, the Environmental Health Index, Finland was rated first followed by Iceland second, Denmark third, Norway fifth and Sweden thirteenth – all of them ahead of the US 16th.[14]

Based on the foregoing surveys, it is not surprising that Nordic people feel secure and happy. This is reflected in the 2019 World Happiness Report, a survey of 156 countries released by the Sustainable Development Solutions Network. In this report, citizens of Finland were rated the world's happiest, followed by Denmark second, Norway third, Iceland fourth and Sweden seventh. The US, by comparison, was rated 19th, a drop of five spots since its 2017 rating.[15]

In the earlier 2018 World Happiness Report, the Gallup World Poll also surveyed the happiness of immigrant populations in a subset of 117 countries. Here too, Nordic countries were solidly in the lead, suggesting that migrants feel included in the culture and benefits of their adopted countries, a result that has enabled them to quickly join the economic and social mainstream. Here again, Finland was rated first, Denmark second, Norway third, and Sweden seventh. Iceland was not rated on this sub-index because it had too few immigrants.

> Perhaps the most striking finding of the whole report is that a ranking of countries according to the happiness of their immigrant populations is almost exactly the same as for the rest of the population. The immigrant happiness rankings are based on the full span of Gallup data from 2005 to 2017.
>
> World Happiness Report, 2018[16]

There is, of course, a feedback loop here. When people feel secure, healthy and happy, they are more inclined to trust and contribute to the welfare of the society in which they exist. As a result, we find interesting correlations with indices on productivity and innovation, where Nordic countries also stand out.

For example, Expert Market (UK) gave Nordic countries top ratings in its 2019 survey on productivity. Measured by GDP per capita in terms of hours worked, Norway rated second, Denmark fourth, Iceland fifth, Sweden sixth and Finland thirteenth. Of particular interest, three Nordic countries moved up between the 2016 and 2019 surveys, with Iceland rising ten notches, Denmark three and Finland one – gains that affirm the quality of their human capital, which is robustly supported by the region's universal health and education policies. While the US was rated seventh on this productivity survey (a solid showing), that result has been thrown into doubt by a 2019 Bloomberg study, which attributed US per capita GDP to aggressive borrowing, without which it would have had a significantly lower result.[17,18]

Because of their leadership in circular economy technologies, Nordic countries are in the top tier of global innovation rankings – in spite of their small economies, which collectively generate only 2% of global GDP. In a 2019 innovation ranking conducted on behalf of Bloomberg, Finland was rated third, Sweden seventh, Denmark eleventh, Norway seventeenth and Iceland twenty-third.[19] In a prior 2018 survey for the World Intellectual Property Organization (WIPO) focused on "breakthrough energy innovations ... essential for global growth and to avert an environmental crisis,"

Sweden was rated third, Finland seventh, Denmark eight and Norway nineteenth.[20] For a region with a small population and limited financial reserves for R&D, this is exceptional performance.

Focus on sustainability and the common good

Because Nordic economies are modeled on living systems, they are naturally drawn to technologies that protect and regenerate life. This proclivity is heightened by a pragmatic awareness that the ecological footprint of global commerce is fast depleting Earth's biological resources. Compared to "big science" technologies that convey national prestige and power, such as advanced physics and space exploration, Nordic R&D is directed primarily toward sustainability.

Following the example of Kalundborg's circular economy innovations noted in Chapter One, Nordic researchers and entrepreneurs have become world leaders in the fields of renewable energy, industrial ecology, bio-innovation and circular economy technologies. The underlying rationale for this work is a shared sense that the world economy is operating far beyond the limits of its biological and mineral resources and that new technologies and business practices are needed to achieve a more sustainable future.

This sense of limits is an important point of departure from the neo-classical model of economics, which treats adverse impacts on Nature and society as "externalities" (matters that are external to the primary goals of growing corporate profits and GDP). To reverse such one-sided practices and restore more balanced methods of accounting, Nordic governments today include in their public reports "indicators for analyzing and integrating environment and economy."[21] Nordic companies do the same, according to a 2017 study by the Boston Consulting Group, by placing environmental, social and governance (ESG) reporting "on a par with financial reporting."[22]

Novo Nordisk, which has been a leader in such advanced accounting, includes in its accounting practices eco-intensity ratios (EIRs), which measure energy and water consumption at every level of production – from R&D to management of its supply chain. Overseen by a team of global "energy stewards," EIR targets are refreshed every year on an annual and long-term basis to ensure continual improvement with the goal of reducing Novo's ecological footprint even as production volume grows. EIRs are also part of a larger integrated system of Environmental Profit and Loss (EPL) accounts that convert into monetary terms metrics such as water use in cubic feet or carbon emissions in tons. Such practices enable Novo to put its environmental impacts on an equal footing with more traditional business/financial concerns. To further embed environmental accounting in Novo's culture, system-wide results are a consideration in the compensation of its CEO.

The values embedded in Nordic accounting systems naturally strengthen their leadership in sustainability practices and innovation. Because companies and governments carefully measure what they want to improve, these accounting practices have supported a surge of activity in renewable energy, bio-innovation and circular economy collaboration.

The high priority Nordic cultures place on such sustainability leadership is clearly visible in the large number of regional corporations named to the world's 100 most sustainable publicly traded companies – an annual survey conducted by Corporate Knights, a Canadian research and publishing company. With less than half of one percent of the world's population, the Nordic region has 37 companies on the Global 100 list for the decade ending in 2019 (details in Appendix Two). Of these, 26 have been listed multiple times and 16 have been listed in the top quartile one or more times. In addition, Nordic companies held the top three rankings for the year 2019. This is an extraordinary record. No other country or region comes close on a per capita basis.

Another indicator of the Nordic region's progressive business ideals is the astonishing success of Helsinki's annual "Slush" event, which has become the world's leading startup venue for entrepreneurs, financiers and others interested in transformative business practices. (The word "Slush" was introduced to differentiate it from Silicon Valley's sunny image and to make light of its launch in early December 2008.) The mission of its student-led founders was "to fix a broken world" by solving "existential threats" through entrepreneurial innovation – an ideal that has drawn a huge global following. Since its first gathering, which attracted roughly 300 attendees, its growth has been explosive. The November 2019 event in Helsinki drew roughly 25,000 attendees from 130 countries, including 3,500 startups, 2,000 investors and 650 journalists. More impressively, Slush gatherings have expanded into Tokyo and Beijing (2015), then to Singapore and Shanghai (2016), and eventually to Nanjing and Shenzhen (2019) where it has addressed record crowds. In addition, informal Slush "small talk" confabs are now held in New York City, London and other global financial centers.[23]

Presenting itself as a "movement" and a "laboratory for new ideas," Slush has become the world's largest network of change entrepreneurs. Its catchy slogans – "We don't want you to learn something. We want you to change something" – resonate with Nordic idealism. To get a sense of the excitement generated by its annual meetings and the dedication of its mostly millennial attendees, readers should visit its website (www.slush.org).

As a result of its rapid growth, Slush now collaborates with Finland's Ministry for Foreign Affairs and diverse global partners in offering a global impact accelerator (GIA). Designed to support impact startups, the accelerator showcases exciting business opportunities in emerging markets that advance the United Nations' Agenda 2030 Sustainable Development Goals (SDGs). In doing so, it also aims to strengthen networks linking "impact actors" in the Nordic community with entrepreneurs in other parts of the world. With a goal of mobilizing capital toward sustainable enterprise and impactful business, this has generated increasing global demand for Nordic expertise and products.

The Nordic Web, founded in 2014, is another offspring of the Slush movement. Each year it generates a list, called the "Nordic 100," of the 100 most impactful and influential figures in the Nordic tech scene each year: "Individuals at the forefront of shaping and positioning the region as one of the world's most important innovation hubs." Its purpose is to generate a community of entrepreneurs, investors and community builders who can collectively generate a more powerful startup system. To accomplish this, in 2017, it created the Nordic Web Angel Fund to "democratize startup investing in the Nordics, allowing the grassroots ecosystem to support the region's strongest companies." The fund provides small initial investments to promising companies then supports them with expert advice, including monthly meetings with an informal advisory board plus full access to a support network through ad hoc online communication and ongoing assistance with hiring, fundraising and problem solving.

European leaders in entrepreneurial startups

Because of such entrepreneurial social capital networks, Nordic countries have become some of the world's most prolific ecosystems for new venture startups. According to Creandum, a leading early-stage venture capital firm, between 2005 and 2015, Nordic countries generated over 7% of global billion-dollar "exits" (the time when original venture investors decide to sell their stakes). Impressively, that was 50% of the total for all of Europe.[24] On the strength of such activity, the Nordic Venture Performance Index (NVPI) generated a nine-fold return for the decade ending in 2016. According to Dealroom, between 2005 and mid-year 2018, they created 12 startups that exceeded the $1 billion valuation (known as "unicorns" due to their rarity) with a combined value of $69 billion.[25] Considered on a per capita basis, that was an outstanding performance.

The value of these successes to Nordic venture capital and startup networks cannot be overstated. With billions of dollars in exit revenue flowing through Nordic economies, people engaged in startups get a morale boost. Employees of successful new companies, emboldened by their experiences, have the economic courage and stability to start new ventures. They get further support from a growing class of cash-rich angel investors eager to maintain the flow of ideas and startup capital.

As the leader of the region's startup success, Stockholm, in 2015, became the world's second most prolific tech hub based on the number of billion-dollar companies created per million people (6.3 versus Silicon Valley's 8.1). Skype became its first unicorn when purchased by eBay for $2.6 billion in 2005, then later repurchased in 2011 by Microsoft for $8.5 billion. Copenhagen in 2016 became the second most prolific entrepreneurial Nordic city for startups, with 98 completed investments (versus 247 for Stockholm).

Copenhagen's Startup Village, a collaboration of more than 40 companies, now calls itself "the largest startup hub in the Nordics." New ventures there can get funding, insight and advice from The Founders Collective, a world-class network of 41 successful Nordic entrepreneurs, venture capitalists and mentors dedicated to "investing in and supporting the next generation of Nordic entrepreneurs with global ambitions." Startups with promising research projects in the fields of life sciences and health care get financial support and advice at all stages of development from the Bio-Innovation Institute, created by the Novo Nordisk Foundation. Copenhagen is also an innovation hub for sustainable energy. By 2016, its Cleantech Cluster project had supported 126 startups and facilitated many additional new partnerships.

Helsinki's rise as a startup hub is catalyzed by two government-directed organizations: Sitra, an independent public foundation that operates under the supervision of the Finnish parliament with an endowment valued at €776 million ($916 million) at yearend 2018, and Business Finland, a public funding agency for research, directed by the Finnish Ministry of Economic Affairs and Employment. Through these organizations, promising startups and investors in sustainable Finnish enterprise can get research grants and loans. The Finnish unicorn, Supercell, infused fresh capital into the system during 2016 when it sold 84.3% of its shares for $8.6 billion to Tencent Holdings, a Chinese multinational investment holding conglomerate.

In addition to such localized sources of funding, the Nordic Investment Bank (NIB) has been an important regional lender to small and medium enterprises (SMEs), which in most countries are underserved by capital markets. Founded in 1976 by the governments of Denmark, Finland, Sweden, Norway and Iceland, its membership was expanded in 2005 to include the governments of Estonia, Latvia and Lithuania. In keeping with the region's progressive, life-affirming policies, its stated mission is to "finance projects that improve productivity and benefit the environment of the Nordic and Baltic countries." In addition, it seeks to "address the needs of the region and the challenges it is facing (including) sustainable growth, technological innovation, climate change, the development of circular economy and the protection of marine environments."[26] By such means, the NIB has facilitated the development of regional strategic networks – clusters of interconnected (symbiotic) companies and institutions in a particular field, much like Kalundborg's biotechnology hub.

With an authorized capital of €6.1 billion and an AAA/Aaa credit rating, the NIB has extensive access to global capital markets, which enables it to lend throughout the Nordic region on favorable terms. Further, by lending in partnership with regional commercial banks, it broadens its strategic reach as it gains detailed knowledge of local conditions. Because of its fastidious screening standards, it remains robustly profitable, a win-win for both the NIB and Nordic economies.

Network synergies

From a systems perspective, these vibrant entrepreneurial and financial networks, plus the Nordic social safety nets that make them possible, generate

important synergies. Because Nordic citizens know that their families'
health, education and future security are protected and because they trust
in the responsibility and fairness of local governance, they are more will-
ing to venture and take risks. In addition, many Nordic people feel a symbiotic urge to give back in ways that create meaning and direction in their
lives. We see this particularly in the expansion of the Slush network into
Asia and in the growing number of Nordic startups that seek to advance the
UN's Sustainable Development Goals.

> Trust promotes economic growth, but it is also a social outcome… In
> the Nordic countries, trust has been generated by delivering relative eco-
> nomic equality and maintaining low levels of corruption. The degree of
> trust in the governance structures, and especially in the legal system,
> also influences mutual trust between people.
>
> Dagfinn Høybråten, Secretary General,
> Nordic Council of Ministers, 2015[27]

These synergetic principles reflect a holistic consciousness and sense of
responsibility embedded in Nordic culture through their education system
– a topic we will explore in the next chapter. This awareness is, in many
ways, the bedrock of their life-mimicking political-economic model as it
invites people to expand their circles of cognitive belonging beyond their
immediate circle of friends and colleagues to Nature, the world at large and
to future generations. In doing so, it endows Nordic people with a capacity
for empathy and systems thinking that reaches past the goal-seeking directives of neoclassical economics. As illustrated in Appendix One, it is one of
the region's primary economic leverage point because it catalyzes so many
other leverage points – from collaborative thinking and information sharing to forward-thinking innovation.

One of these leverage points is the earlier mentioned Nordic practice of
managing by means (MBM). Understanding that healthy people and ecosystems are the means by which countries and companies create durable
value and progress, Nordic political-economic leaders place high priorities
on practices that optimize human and ecological resources. Importantly,
these include maintaining the region's universal safety nets, advancing its
circular economy practices and promoting total cost accounting systems –
qualities that tangibly feedback to higher productivity.

Compared to the more conventional practice of managing by results (MBR), where the pursuit of profit and GDP often subvert the well-being of people and Nature, Nordic MBM practices yield consistently better results as will be shown in later chapters.

This is an important distinction in understanding the integrity and power of the life-mimicking Nordic Model. As we look more deeply into its inner workings, we will see more clearly why it is so productive and why the rival neoclassical model is locked in a downward spiral of ecological degradation, debt and divisiveness. Based on the evidence at hand, there is no question which model is best for humanity and the planet.

Notes

1   Robert D Putnam. 1993. *Making Democracy Work*. Princeton, NJ: Princeton University Press, p. 167.
2   Michael Porter. 2015. "Why the social progress index is the best metric of national performance," *Huffpost*. June 9. Available from: https://www. huffingtonpost.com/michael-porter/social-progress-index_b_7034130.ht ml [Accessed June 29, 2020].
3   Francis Fukuyama. 1995. *Trust: The Social Virtues and the Creation of Prosperity*. New York: The Free Press.
4   Stephen Knack and Philip Keefer. 1997. "Does social capital have an economic payoff?" *Quarterly Journal of Economics*. 12(4): p. 1283.
5   Sjoerd Beugelsdijk et al. 2004. "Trust and economic growth: a robust analysis," *Oxford Economic Papers*. 56(1): pp. 118–34.
6   Christian Bjørnskov. 2017. "Social trust and economic growth," In Uslaner EM, ed. *Oxford Handbook of Social and Political Trust*. Available from: http:// dx.doi.org/10.2139/ssrn.2906280. p. 13.
7   The Social Progress Imperative. 2018. "Index to action to impact," *The Social Progress Imperative*. Available from: https://www.socialprogress.org /index/global/results [Accessed June 29, 2020].
8   The Legatum Institute. 2020. "The Legatum Prosperity Index 2019," Prosperity.com. Available from: https://www.prosperity.com/rankings [Accessed June 29, 2020].
9   The Legatum Institute. 2017. "Distinct models of success: Nordics and the anglosphere," Prosperity.com. November 29. Available from: http://www. prosperity.com/feed/Distinct-models-of-success-Nordics-and-the-Anglosphere [Accessed June 29, 2020].
10 Klaus Boehnke and Jan Dehley. 2013. "Measuring common ground – an international comparison of social cohesion." Bertelsmann Stiftung Foundation. Available from: http://www.ires.piemonte.it/pdf/coesione-soci ale-radar.pdf [Accessed June 29, 2020].

11   C Capretta. 2018. "Opinion: the financial hole for social security and medicare is even deeper than the experts say," *MarketWatch*. June 16. Available from: https://www.marketwatch.com/story/the-financial-hole-for-social-security-and-medicare-is-even-deeper-than-the-experts-say-2018-06-15 [Accessed June 29, 2020].

12   Natixis Investment Managers. 2019. "2019 global retirement index," *Natixis Investment Managers*. Available from: https://www.im.natixis.com/us/resources/global-retirement-index-2019-report [Accessed June 29, 2020].

13   Fund For Peace. 2019. "Fragile states index annual report 2019," *FFP*. Available from: https://fundforpeace.org/wp-content/uploads/2019/04/9511904-fragilestatesindex.pdf [Accessed June 29, 2020].

14   Environmental Performance Index. 2020. "Environmental health results," *EPI*. Available from: https://epi.envirocenter.yale.edu/epi-indicator-report/HLT [Accessed June 29, 2020].

15   World Happiness Report. 2019. *World Happiness Report*. March 20. Available from: https://worldhappiness.report/ed/2019/ [Accessed June 29, 2020].

16   World Happiness Report. 2018. *World Happiness Report 2018*. March 14. Available from: http://worldhappiness.report/ed/2018/ [Accessed June 29, 2020].

17   Robb Bins. "The world's most productive countries and how to replicate at work." Expert Market Co. (updated July 24, 2020). Available from: https://www.expertmarket.co.uk/crm-systems/the-ultimate-guide-to-work-place-productivity

18   V Del Giudice and W Lu. 2019. "America's wealth hinges on its ability to borrow big – or else," *Bloomberg*. August 31. Available from: https://www.bloomberg.com/news/articles/2019-08-31/america-s-wealth-hinges-on-its-ability-to-borrow-big-or-else [Accessed June 29, 2020].

19   Michelle Jamrisco and Wei Lu. 2020. *Bloomberg Innovation Index*. January 18. Available from: https://datawrapper.dwcdn.net/3hi4O/2/?abcnewsembedheight=550

20   Cornell University, INSEAD, WIPO. 2018. *Global Innovation Index. 2018*. Available from: https://www.wipo.int/pressroom/en/articles/2018/article_0005.html

21   Olle Björk et al. 2016. "Making the environment count," *TemaNord* 2016:507. Available from: https://norden.diva-portal.org/smash/get/diva2:915431/fulltext01.pdf

22   Douglas Beal et al. 2019. "What companies can learn from world leaders in societal impact," *Boston Consulting Group*. April 23. https://www.bcg.com/en-us/publications/2019/world-leaders-social-impact.aspx

23   Small Talks. 2019. "Impact New York." West Edge, Chelsea. June 27, 2019. *Slush*. Available from: https://www.slush.org/small-talks/new-york-2019/

24   Creandum Nordic Tech Exit Report 2016. Available from: https://www.dropbox.com/s/4v5mli29ptfde3f/Creandum%20Nordic%20Exit%20Analysis%202016_v4%20%281%29.pdf?dl=0 [Accessed June 29, 2020].

25   TECHBBQ and Dealroom.co. "Nordic venture capital report," September 25, 2018. https://blog.dealroom.co/wp-content/uploads/2018/09/BBQ-vLong.pdf

26   Nordic Investment Bank: Financing the Future. https://www.nib.int/who_we_are/about

27   Dagfinn Høybråten. 2015. "Trust behind Nordic success," *Huffington Post*. January 17. Available from: https://www.huffingtonpost.com/dagfinn-hoybraten/trust-behind-nordic-succe_b_6170250.html [Accessed June 29, 2020].

3

THE CATALYTIC POWER OF EDUCATION

Learning organizations are where people continually expand their capacity to create the results they truly desire, where new and expansive patterns of thinking are nurtured, where collective aspiration is set free, and where people are continually learning how to learn together.

Peter Senge[1]

[A] growing body of empirical research suggests that better education yields higher individual income and contributes towards the construction of social capital and long-term economic growth.

Our World in Data[2]

In the mid-19th century, a new philosophy of education evolved in Scandinavia that elevated it in the space of three generations from one of the poorest, least developed areas in Europe to one of the most prosperous. By providing "school for all" at public expense, that system today keeps Nordic people at or near the top of global surveys on education, human capital, productivity and economic progress.

The wonderful thing about this Nordic approach is how it invites students and adult learners to reflect and think systemically: beyond a particular subject to the interests, experiences and worldviews they bring to learning. In the early years of education, this starts with a respectful dialogue between student and teacher, where students are encouraged to question assumptions and to think independently. By bringing their whole selves into the learning process, this method eventually "brings forth" a love of learning and exploration that eventually takes on a life of its own. While some may question this approach as lacking specific pedagogic focus, it is hard to question the results.

According to the International Education Database (IED), which rates national education systems in support of the UN's Sustainable Development Goals, the four largest Nordic countries were all rated in the top ten of its 2019 survey. Out of more than 200 countries evaluated, Finland was ranked first, Denmark third, Sweden seventh, Norway ninth and Iceland thirtieth – all matching or improving their prior year standings.[3]

Within this group, Finland is a fascinating story. Following its break from Russia in 1917 plus the hardships of two world wars, it began to transform its education system in the 1970s as part of an economic recovery plan. By the year 2000, Finnish 15-year-olds ranked first for reading in the Program for International Student Assessment (PISA) tests. By 2003 they led in math. And by 2006, they were first in science. Today 93% of Finns graduate from academic or vocational high schools (17.5 percentage points higher than the United States) and 66% go on to higher education – the highest rate in the European Union. In spite of this, Finland spends 30% less per student than the United States. One of the keys to its success is that schooling starts early. Finland provides three years of maternity leave and subsidized daycare to parents plus preschool for all five-year-olds, where the emphasis is on play and socializing. By the age of six, virtually all children have begun academic study. Schools provide food, counseling and taxi service if needed. Student health care is free.[4]

As will be seen throughout this book, such results are threads in the fabric of an ongoing story of human development. Consider, for example, the UN's 2019 Human Development Index, a survey of 189 countries and territories. Based on expected and mean years of schooling, life expectancy at birth and gross national income per capita at purchase price parity, Nordic countries were solidly ranked in the top decile with Norway first, Iceland sixth, Sweden eighth, Denmark eleventh and Finland twelfth – all ahead of the US fifteenth.[5]

There is a pattern here. Human capital and productivity correlate more closely with the quality of education and human talent than with the scale of a country's economic resources. As evidence, it is interesting to note that Iceland, with a population of only 335,000, is rated above the US on productivity, as mentioned in the Expert Market productivity survey (Chapter Two). The difference appears to be that Iceland's talent is widespread due to the country's egalitarian approach to education and training whereas productivity in the US is based on a select group of highly compensated talent.

The Nordic Secret

The philosophy of education that transformed Scandinavia into the productivity and innovation power center it is today is remarkably simple. Based on the concept of education for all from preschool onward, it ensures that anyone who wants to develop knowledge and skills has the opportunity to do so at public expense. Called "folk Bildung," it works by progressively widening an individual's circle of belonging: from narrow self-interests toward a holistic caring for Nature and the wellbeing of others; a love of democracy in one's own country and abroad and a concern for future generations. While not everyone goes to the outer edges of this circle, the ideals of Bildung are embedded enough in Nordic civilization that the region has become a center of sustainable innovation for the world, as indicated in Chapter Two.

As an ideal, folk Bildung is rooted in the philosophies of the 17th- and 18th-century Enlightenment and the 19th-century progressive movement – a time when Northern European people were trying to break free from older feudal norms that limited their possibilities in life. This does not mean it is exclusive to people of European origin. Rather, it is an expression of the human desire for self-improvement, which exists everywhere.

The story of Nordic countries' journey toward the positions they currently hold as global exemplars of freedom, democracy, prosperity and progress is brilliantly distilled by Lene Rachel Andersen and Tomas Björkman in their book, The Nordic Secret. For anyone wishing to know why Nordic economies today outperform those operating under the older neoclassical model, this is required reading.[6]

As a method of teaching, folk Bildung became a force in Scandinavian education in the 1850s when Christen Kold, an idealistic young Danish teacher, introduced it as a means of engaging the natural curiosity of children. Unlike the more traditional method of rote learning, Kold drew his students into learning through respectful dialogue. As they progressed, he urged them to question assumptions, to value Nature and democracy and to take responsibility for becoming enlightened, productive citizens.

In keeping with the progressive ideals of Northern Europe during the 19th-century, folk Bildung was premised on beliefs that all people are born equal, that they have a natural desire to make the most of their abilities and that they find meaning in contributing to the greater good of their communities, countries and cultures. Therefore, by making education available to all children, it would generate upward mobility to the benefit of all.

The origin of the word Bildung conveys its higher meaning. In its earliest use, it meant shaping oneself in God's image (Bild). Its later secular meaning, by which it is known today, conveys popular ideals concerning freedom, democracy, self-development and self-cultivation – the means by which people take control of their lives.

> *Bildung* is the combination of cultivation, enculturation and moral, emotional and personal development. It is character formation, cultural heritage and developing a moral backbone all in one. Bildung is consciousness and conscience, awareness and responsibility, and it is a lifelong learning process and maturation of our mind.
>
> Lene Rachael Andersen[7]

In telling this story, Andersen and Björkman refer to the ideals of eminent philosophers whose popular works raised expectations of a more meaningful human existence. Among these were the social contract theories of John Locke, David Hume and Jean Jacques Rousseau, which inspired people to believe that the legitimacy of government rested on the consent of those governed: that citizens could become freer and more independent through education and reflection. The ideals of Anthony Ashley-Cooper, England's third Earl of Shaftesbury, were also widely influential – especially his moral sense of "virtue for its own sake" which directed people to "harmonize with Nature; and live in Friendship with both GOD and Man."[8]

As the 18th-century Enlightenment gave way to the progressive era of the 19th-century and the emerging industrial revolution, other philosophers invested *Bildung* with new meaning. Foremost among these was Immanuel Kant, who held that we create our own realities through our *"a priori"* mental models of the world – models that determine how we see and experience it and how we might, thereby, modify it. His ideals, in turn, influenced progressive thinkers like Johann Fichte and Georg Hegel, who believed that advancement was a continual process that spread from generation to generation through the improvement of knowledge. Writing at the time of the American and French Revolutions, when the ideals of freedom and democracy were rampant, all three men developed avid followers in the Nordic world.

Up to this time, the primary focus of *Bildung* was on developing individual consciousness and will through education. Ethical questions of *conscience*, social responsibility and caring for the poor were largely unaddressed. That changed, however, under the influence of the Swiss teacher and author Johann Pestalozzi, whose ideal of *Burgerliche Bildung* (civic *Bildung*) advanced an egalitarian approach to education in which all children, especially the poor, would be served. Moved by Hegel's vision of progress, Pestalozzi's approach was to engage the "heads, hands and hearts" of children by inviting them to participate in the learning process so they might become independent citizens with moral senses of responsibility.

Among those inspired by Pestalozzi's ideals and teaching methods was Wilhelm von Humboldt, who in 1809 became Prussia's minister of education. He famously reformed Prussia's school and university systems by giving students the freedom to choose their own courses of study once they had developed their powers of reasoning. This break from older teaching methods, which were rooted in authority and dogma, became part of the new German humanism (*Neuhumanismus*). By developing the intellectual, physical and moral formation of a "better human being," Humboldt believed Prussia would be strengthened by a growing educated middle class. In addition, he believed that education should be a life-long process of human development, rather than mere training in gaining practical knowledge and skills – a core principle of *Bildung* that remains strongly embedded in Nordic culture today.

The movement that later became known as *folk Bildung* originated in 1850 at a folk high school in Ryslinge, Denmark, where Christen Kold, whose teaching was inspired by Pestalozzi and Humboldt, began to engage students as equals through storytelling and dialogue. With the industrial revolution moving ahead at increasing speed via railroads, telegraph and mechanized factories, Kold's goal was to develop students into self-confident citizens with curiosity and practical skills based on the latest knowledge. His approach, which was both pragmatic and respectful, became an instant hit and spread rapidly throughout the region.

By the 1880s, folk Bildung was the norm throughout Scandinavia. As described by Andersen and Björkman, it "turned tens of thousands of young people into inspired, self-governing young adults with a purpose... to do what was good for themselves, their local community and their country."[9] Over the next few decades, as it moved from rural areas into the cities, it evolved toward more diverse programs in literature, science, culture, politics and sports – qualities that gave students a deeper sense of cultural belonging in their communities.

As these students entered adulthood, this sense of affiliation coalesced into self-organizing movements to improve their communities through civic, cultural and entrepreneurial collaborations. During this time, Scandinavian economies transitioned rapidly toward industrialization catalyzed by large infrastructure projects (railroads, electrification, telegraph), which linked and energized the growing fields of mining, forestry, finance, engineering and mechanized manufacturing. Between 1850 and 1870, Sweden had the world's second-highest economic growth rate after Japan.

One of the most memorable people to emerge during this late 19th-century take-off period was Alfred Nobel. Born in Stockholm in 1833, he entered adulthood as folk Bildung was spreading throughout Scandinavia. During his life as one of Europe's most successful entrepreneurs, he became widely read in diverse subjects, including Humboldt's theory of knowledge. Moved by Bildung ideals of "self-improvement" and "self-cultivation," he became fluent in five languages, wrote plays and poetry and was active in social and peace-related issues. Upon his death in 1896, his estate, which was donated "for the Greatest Benefit to Mankind," became the foundation for the famed Nobel prizes in literature, physics, chemistry, medicine, peace and economics.

Accelerating economic development

Looking back over the trajectory of Nordic economies since the educational reforms of folk Bildung, it is astonishing how quickly these changes boosted their standards of living. Although Sweden had the fastest growth record, Denmark and Norway were also highly developed by the 1930s. Finland took longer because it was a Grand Duchy of Imperial Russia until 1917, following which it was disrupted by two world wars. Nevertheless, its long-standing connections to the folk Bildung movements of its Nordic neighbors enabled it to catch up rapidly in the post-World-War-II era.

The swift development of Nordic economies in the 20th century parallels the expanding consciousness of their people. As their shared "circles of belonging" widened, they developed a capacity to see and understand the world in a broad holistic context and to respond proactively to emerging economic challenges. The common thread in these wide circles of engagement is respect for life: a value rooted in Pestalozzi's ethics and Shaftesbury's vision of living in "harmony with Nature."

The eminent Harvard socio-biologist Edward O. Wilson later named this very human instinct "biophilia," which he defined as an innate human tendency to focus on life and life-like processes. In his 1986 book, titled Biophilia, he described how these qualities became wired into the human genome over thousands of generations: because individuals who revered life lived longer than those who did not and were therefore better able to pass on their genes.[10]

Since Wilson's definitive work, a growing school of thought has coalesced around the connections between humanity's biophilic instincts and our highest "spiritual intelligence" (SQ). To physicist Danah Zohar, who coined the term "spiritual intelligence," people who think and act in accord with such instincts engage their highest thinking capacities, which give meaning and direction to their other intelligences, including their aptitudes for creativity and innovation.[11] Doubt it, if you will, but the elevated SQ of Nordic people has endowed them with exceptional capacities for creativity and sustainable innovation.

As evidence of this, consider the Global Sustainability Competitiveness Index, an annual survey of 180 countries based on five variables: governance, intellectual capital, natural capital, social capital and resource efficiency. Compiled by SolAbility, a global think tank and advisory founded in 2005, its rankings are based on data made available by the World Bank, the International Monetary Fund (IMF), diverse UN agencies and prominent NGOs. Similar to other global surveys cited in this book, its 2019 rankings placed Sweden at the top for global sustainability competitiveness, followed by Finland (2), Iceland (3), Denmark (4), Switzerland (5) and Norway (6).[12]

Although holding less than half of one percent of the world's population, Nordic countries were also rated in the top tier of the 2015 Global Creativity Index (GCI) sponsored by the World Economic Forum. Of the 139 nations surveyed, the Nordic five were solidly in the top decile with Denmark and Finland tied for fifth, followed closely by Sweden (7), Iceland (8) and Norway (11).[13] We find similar top echelon results in the 2018 Global Innovation Index compiled by the World Intellectual Property Organization (WIPO), as mentioned in Chapter Two.

What we see in these connections is a feedback loop where high-quality education and Nordic SQ strengthen regional economic development, and where that development in turn supports free public education as it feeds through to government revenues.

> "What made the Nordic countries successful were not unique natural resources or some magic ingredient that cannot be reproduced somewhere else, it was human development and cultivation."
>
> Andersen and Björkman, 2017[14]

A word of caution

Andersen and Björkman wisely accompany their endorsement of *Bildung* with a word of caution. Their primary concern is that the original teaching methods of *folk Bildung* have become diluted by school curricula designed to achieve high PISA test scores in preference to those grounded in Nordic culture. Consequently, they warn that: "As the world becomes increasingly complex, we are making education still narrower."[15]

While this concern is worth heeding, it should also be noted that the cultural values of human societies are subject to cycles in the same way that ecosystems are. Those founded on durable life-affirming principles have an inner capacity to right themselves when they lose their balance. (This is what systems thinkers call a "balancing loop" because it redirects energy back to restoring fundamental values.) In America, the Declaration of Independence, like *Bildung*, is a compass point of immense cultural value that has inspired great effort and progress. In spite of this, over the past two centuries, the Declaration has been periodically challenged by events.

To resolve such challenges, the US has fought a civil war, expanded voting rights, created regulations on corporate over-reach and forced a sitting president out of office. Importantly, as the nation struggled through each challenge, it found new strength. Who, in the year 2000, could have imagined the inauguration of Barack Obama, its first black president, or the spread of US democratic ideals as transformative models for change in leading American companies?[16]

Even the presidency of Donald Trump, which today seems a step backward toward oligarchy, is another such wake-up call – one that is meeting resistance from state and local governments, the courts, the free press and popular demonstrations. In a Pew Research poll published in April 2018 amidst the rising chaos of his presidency, an overwhelming share of the public (84%) said it is very important that "the rights and freedoms of all people are respected." Nearly as many 73% also said the phrase "people are free to peacefully protest" describes this country very or somewhat well. In addition, an overwhelming majority (77%) supports limits on the amount of money individuals and organizations can spend on political campaigns and issues. And nearly two-thirds (65%) say new laws could be effective in reducing the role of money in politics.[17] As further evidence of Americans' regard for the nation's founding principles, the November 2018 elections indicated a shift in public sentiment: a strong rejection of oligarchy and centralized power. In other words, even though US freedoms have been under assault by a president and vested interests that would dilute them, the ideals of the Declaration remain firmly embedded in American values.

There is likewise broad public support for the ideals of Bildung in Nordic culture. Although they may not be the subject of everyday conversation, they too are deeply embedded and respected. The word Bildung itself has been used by the Nordic Council of Ministers to stimulate discussion in the field of education. In 2018, for example, it sponsored in collaboration with local universities, a regional study circle on "Learning and Bildung in Times of Globalization."[18] In 2014 it also sponsored the Biophilia Education Project created for schoolchildren between the ages of 11 and 12. Modeled on Bildung, the project's approach was to use creativity as a teaching and research tool by linking together subjects that actively interest students – music, technology and the natural world – in ways that encourage them to learn in a "space of exchange and debate … (with) room for personal and social growth." Like folk *Bildung*, the project's long-term goal was to develop "more highly conscious societies."[19]

In launching both explorations into *Bildung*, the Nordic Council of Ministers appear to agree with Andersen and Björkman that this seminal philosophy must remain a centerpiece of Nordic culture. Having been immersed in this learning philosophy themselves, the ministers understand its links to the high quality of life in Nordic countries.

So what is it about *Bildung* that enables Nordic political-economic leaders and entrepreneurs to out-think their peers in countries where decision-making power is more hierarchical and centralized? Could it be how they perceive the world through their mental models, as Kant suggests? Could it be the assumptions they bring into learning or how they approach "learning about learning'" as envisioned by the previously mentioned Biophilia Education Project?

More than any technology, this ability to keep asking questions, testing assumptions and challenging old paradigms, appears to be the way forward. The US, with its huge industrial economy and the technical prowess of Silicon Valley, today lags behind the Nordic world in this one crucial talent, which helps to explain why the US economy is today so politically fraught, indebted and vulnerable.

Nordic skill at double- and triple-loop learning

One of the key strengths of the Nordic education system is that it invites people to imagine the world in a global symbiotic (eco-centered) context rather than in a more parochial (ego-centered) one. This, of course, opens vast new fields of inquiry, which lead to deeper thought and expanded realms of possibility. In essence, such deep learning looks beyond data to the assumptions we use in analyzing data (double loop) and to our very methods of learning itself (triple loop).

In the field of economics, single-loop learning follows set rules, primarily those focused on optimizing gross domestic product (GDP). This is the Achille's heel of the GDP-focused neoclassical model, which too often excludes from reality adverse feedback, such as climate change.

With double-loop learning, we question operating premises whenever they cease to work as expected, with the goal of changing our rules of engagement. This is what Nordic countries did in the early 1990s when they famously reformed their deficit spending practices and returned to balanced budget regimes.

Triple-loop learning goes a step further to reflect on whether we are asking the right questions about a future we may not yet fully understand – a relatively new approach to economics that invites us to think more deeply about our relationships with the whole of life, which is the primary source of our wellbeing.

One way to crystalize the difference between these approaches to learning is to observe how the US and Nordic countries have managed their sovereign debt over recent decades – particularly in situations, like now, when debt levels threaten social and ecological wellbeing around the world. This is germane because the amount of debt countries accumulate relative to their GDP is based on factual accounting data rather than more subjective discussions about ecological risk, climate change and quality of life.

Since 1980, US federal debt has grown faster than its GDP in all but a few years, as shown in Appendix Four. Although correlation is not causation, this fact parallels the growth of ecological overstep and climate change, which mainstream neoclassical economists generally choose to ignore. Too often overlooked, there is a negative feedback loop here: the more we degrade the web of life that underpins the US and world economies, the more our political-economic leaders borrow to rescue the system from failure. Yet the more they borrow, the more social and ecological risks they take in order to relieve their debt burdens. In systems thinking terms, this has become a self-reinforcing downward spiral.

At the end of its September 2019 fiscal year, US government debt was $22.7 trillion versus GDP of roughly $21.4 trillion, suggesting a debt/GDP ratio in the vicinity of 106 percent. To place this in perspective, that ratio was more than triple what it was in 1980 and 67% higher than at the start of the 2007/8 recession.

When the debts of state and local governments ($3.1 trillion) and US households ($39 trillion) are taken into consideration, the ratio of US credit market debt to GDP exceeded three to one at yearend 2019. When the implicit debt of federal and state unfunded liabilities are further included, the total debt burden at yearend 2019 was in the vicinity of $100 trillion to $180 trillion, depending on the actuarial assumptions used to assess those liabilities. Consequently, however one chooses to reckon this debt burden, it was five or more times larger than GDP and growing at a substantially faster pace.

The danger of this predicament was made worse by the 2020 coronavirus pandemic, which rapidly inflated debt at all levels. As economic activity slowed due to public-health-related business shut-downs, the debt-carrying capacity of the US economy sharply declined. Although Nordic economies faced similar problems, these were easier to manage because Nordic public health systems were better, their universal safety nets more efficient and their debt-carrying capacities stronger due to their low sovereign debt ratios.

In spite of these increasingly obvious differences, most US economists refuse to question their assumptions. Instead, they address the country's debt problems as one of liquidity, which they approach by borrowing (and printing) more money. As illustrated in Appendix Four, this has become a lose-lose spiral that erodes trust and ultimately places the US economy at grave risk.

By comparison, when Nordic countries faced a difficult budget crisis in the early 1990s, they did the exact opposite. Rather than trying to borrow their way out of debt, they quickly addressed the flaws in their budgeting processes and the risks their high debt ratios posed to their universal safety nets and future productivity.

Thanks to their capacities for systems thinking and multiple-loop learning, they were quick to see the flaws in their fiscal budgeting. Therefore, instead of doubling down on debt and continuing business as usual, they transparently questioned all spending priorities and quickly rationalized their budgets. Because of this proactive response, Nordic governments have run more budget surpluses than deficits since the 1990s. Consequently, in spite of offering their citizens some of the world's most generous social safety nets, their sovereign debt ratios are today substantially lower than the US and the European Union average (details in Chapter Four).

Holistic thinking: A path to the future

The economic advantages Nordic economies enjoy today are due to their capacities for holistic systems thinking. Described in terms of folk Bildung, Nordic people have expanded their conscious circles of belonging: beyond themselves and their communities to their relationships with Nature, their associations with the larger community of nations and their legacies to future generations.

In doing so, they implicitly recognize that human economies are sub-systems of life (a core assumption that the neoclassical school ignores). Consequently, they are drawn to political-economic systems modeled on the structures and symbiotic methods of Nature. This eco-centric mind-set, which imagines productivity in terms of healthy people and a healthy planet, as we shall see, is far more effective than the neoclassical (ego-centric) one where powerful people exploit Nature and their fellows in their quests for wealth, power and GDP.

Inviting as this eco-centric vision sounds, its egalitarian, co-operative mindset does not come easily to countries with a history of imperial power and entitlement. When humanity evolved as a species roughly 200,000 years ago, the keys to survival were being strong, aggressive and alert. At the beginning of recorded history 5,500 years ago, people lived in clans and tribes that often fought with one another for domination and control. These genes remain deeply embedded in us today, along with the more life-affirming genes that inform our biophilic instincts and collaborative behaviors.

The challenge we now face is how to reconcile these opposing instinc-tive urges in a crowded world with depleting natural resources. As we awaken to the realities that infinite growth on a finite planet is impossible and that hyper-competitive economic and business strategies are destroy-ing the Earth's biological carrying capacity, we have begun to realize that we need a new way forward – one that enables us to live and work more harmoniously with Nature and each other.

Although few people in mid-19th-century Scandinavia could imagine the dilemmas of the 21st-century world economy, they developed a philos-ophy of education and a way of life that enabled them to learn and adapt as conditions change. With the world population today roughly seven times larger than it was in 1850 and a global economy operating at nearly double Earth's biological carrying capacity, this philosophy is more than a means of thriving. It has become, in fact, a matter of survival.

Looking beyond the Nordic world, it is encouraging to note that other countries have adopted key elements of their life-mimicking worldview and strategy. This includes European countries that participated in the early development of *Bildung* (Austria, Belgium, Germany, Holland, Switzerland,

UK) plus those with progressive learning cultures (Ireland, Canada, Australia, New Zealand, Singapore and South Korea). In virtually all global surveys on quality of education and sustainable economic progress, these countries are clustered near the top with the Nordic five. By democratizing education and teaching people to think systemically, they have greatly strengthened their political-economic systems.

That said, Bildung is not a destination, but a path to the future. Because life and relationships are continually in flux, the best we can do is listen to what the system tells us. Consequently, learning to live and work in harmony with the rest of life cannot be defined by fixed rules. Rather, it is a process of continuous attentiveness, questioning assumptions when confronted by negative feedback (such as climate change, ecosystem degradation) and even questioning our learning methods themselves (when systems can no longer be understood in terms of familiar concepts). While this sounds daunting, it works as Nordic countries have shown us from Kalundborg to the present day.

In the final analysis, just as people have a capacity to rewire their brains, countries do too. Although Nordic countries got a head start through the development of folk Bildung, its progressive, egalitarian methods can be learned anywhere because they engage our shared humanity and our dreams for a better future. To authors Andersen and Björkman, that is its magic. And its promise for the future.

Notes

1 Peter S Senge. 1990. *The Fifth Discipline – The Art and Practice of the Learning Organization*. New York: Doubleday. p. 1.
2 https://ourworldindata.org/global-rise-of-education
3 The World Top 20 Project. 2019. https://worldtop20.org/education-database-2019
4 LynNell Hancock. "Why are Finland's schools successful?" *Smithsonian Magazine* . September 2011. Available from: http://www.smithsonianmag .com/innovation/why-are-finlands-schools-successful-49859555/
5 Human Development Reports 2019. United Nations Development Programme. http://hdr.undp.org/en/content/2019-human-development-index-ranking
6 Lene Rachel Andersen and Thomas Björkman. 2017. *The Nordic Secret*. Stockholm: Fri Tanke.
7 https://nordicbildung.org/folk-bildung/

8 Andersen and Björkman, *The Nordic Secret*, p. 83.

9 Op. Cit. Andersen and Björkman, *The Nordic Secret*, p. 271.

10 Edward O Wilson. 1986. *Biophilia*. Cambridge: Harvard University Press.

11 Danah Zohar and Ian Marshall. 2000. *Spiritual Intelligence: The Ultimate Intelligence*. London: Bloomsbury Publishing.

12 SolAbility. *The Global Sustainable Compeitive Index 2019*. Available from: The-Global-Sustainable-Competitiveness-Index-2019.pdf

13 Martin Prosperity Institute (University of Toronto). *The Global Creativity Index 2015*. Available from: http://martinprosperity.org/media/Global-Creativity-Index-2015.pdf

14 Op. Cit. Andersen and Björkman, *The Nordic Secret*, p. 382.

15 Op. Cit. Andersen and Björkman, *The Nordic Secret*, p. 350.

16 For case histories on the democratization of US and global corporations, see: Joseph H Bragdon. 2016. *Companies that Mimic Life*. Oxfordshire: Routledge.

17 Pew Research Center. 2018. "The public, the political system and american democracy." Available from: http://www.people-press.org/2018/04/26/the-public-the-political-system-and-american-democracy/

18 Nordic Summer University. *Learning and Bildung in Times of Globalization. CfP Summer Session 2018*. Available from: http://nordic.university/study-circles/8-learning-bildung-times-globalisation/

19 Faena Group. *Biophilia: A Revolutionary Educational Project by Bjork*. Available from: http://www.faena.com/aleph/articles/biophilia-a-revolutionary-educational-project-by-bjork/

4

FRUGALITY AS STRENGTH

Lagom är bäst (The right amount is best.)

Swedish Proverb

"Our mission is Creation of Sustainable Economic Growth via creating good quality, accessible and affordable solutions."

Nordic Frugal Innovation Society, 2013[1]

Sweden, one of the world's most prosperous countries, recycles more than 99% of its household waste, which is separated, then used to generate district heating, electricity, biogas, fertilizer and other materials. The ash from the portion that is burned yields diverse metals for further recycling plus gravel that is used for road building; less than 1% of the original waste volume is deposited in landfill.[2]

Sweden has become so good at extracting value from household waste that it now imports waste from the UK, Italy, Norway and Ireland to feed its 34 waste-to-energy (WTE) plants. The rationale for doing this is clear. In these plants, four tonnes of waste yield as much energy as one tonne of fuel oil. Consequently, if Sweden burns two million tonnes of waste per year, it gets approximately the same energy as 500,000 tonnes of fuel oil – energy that it uses to generate electricity and run its efficient district heating systems.

This frugal closed-loop process enables Sweden to generate a substantial amount of the energy and material it needs to support its advanced economy while also lowering its ecological footprint. Similar to Kalundborg, which pioneered recycling industrial waste and by-products into energy and useful materials (as discussed in Chapter One), Sweden is at the front of a household recycling revolution that saves money and supports a healthy, abundant lifestyle for its citizens.

In terms of the six attributes of economies that mimic life summarized in Table 1.1, this recycling practice replicates the efficiency of Nature where waste and decay become food for diverse species whose wellbeing and exchanges of value keep the system in a healthy balance. The primary difference is that the exchange system in Nature is spontaneous, whereas in progressive life-mimicking economies, it is based on conscious human choice.

To Nordic people, that choice is informed by a holistic philosophy of education (described in Chapter Three), which endows citizens with a capacity for systems thinking: an understanding that the health of a community, business or nation depends on the health of the whole system. Considered in this context, frugality feeds a reinforcing loop. By reducing and recycling waste in ways that reinforce the health of people and Nature, the system thrives and gains resilience.

Nordic social capital networks described in Chapter Two play an important role in this dynamic, amplified by a shared awareness that we live in a world of limited and increasingly scarce resources, which makes thrift, sharing and collaboration a necessity, even a heroic enterprise.

That awareness, as noted in Chapter Two, is ubiquitous at Helsinki's student-led annual Slush events, whose unifying themes embrace "how entrepreneurs can tackle the world's problems." As the world's leading startup event, it draws entrepreneurs and investors committed to sustainable business practices, often with the express purpose of advancing the United Nations' eco-centric Sustainable Development Goals (SDGs). The global popularity of these events is such that Sitra, the government-sponsored Finnish innovation fund, collaborates with Slush in producing circular

economy workshops and global impact accelerators for startups in developing countries, all of which create opportunities for partnering with Finnish
companies and those from its Nordic neighbors.[3]

The non-profit Nordic Frugal Innovation Society (TNFIS) also partners
in such collaborations. As the world's first non-profit to focus exclusively
on frugal innovation, it is dedicated to developing "frugal ecosystems" in
Nordic and emerging markets. Working with diverse global cohorts, it seeks
to "reduce inequality via sustainable economic growth" by promoting circular economy methods, open innovation, lean methodologies, biodesign and
social enterprise by matchmaking startups, non-profits and impact funds.

Beyond such extensions of Nordic support to circular economy enterprise, the movement has been joined by the Ellen MacArthur Foundation,
the UN and the World Circular Economy Forum (created in 2017 by Sitra).
By this reckoning, what started in Kalundborg during the 1970s has become
a rising tide of new thinking and enterprise.

Interestingly, as this frugal eco-centric movement becomes more global,
Nordic countries remain in the creative vanguard. By contrast, other industrial countries, although eager to explore circular economy opportunities,
remain hamstrung by their neoclassical models, which remain wedded
to fossil fuels and related power structures. Like the US, their mainstream
political-economic leaders therefore tend to regard circular economy strategies as methods of plugging holes in their deficient systems rather than
reinventing their systems organically from the bottom up.

Challenging conventional wisdom: circular versus linear

Framed as such, Nordic economies continue to challenge the operating
premises of the neoclassical model. Instead of prioritizing ends (GDP and
profit growth), a linear process that often overrides the wellbeing of people
and Nature, they use a circular process that aims to strengthen people and
Nature because these are the primary sources of sustainable value creation.
In addition, rather than discounting damage done to human health, infrastructure and ecosystems as "externalities," which mainstream economists
routinely do, Nordic accounting systems recognize their impacts on Nature
and society.

The dichotomy between the two models reflects a fundamental disagree-
ment on the idea of growth itself. To Nordic political-economic leaders,

infinite consumption on a finite planet is impossible, which means the only way we can live sustainably on Earth is to be frugal in our use of biological and mineral resources.

The neoclassical model, however, believes that continuous consumption growth is possible because advances in technology will eventually overcome systemic disruptions. Although intellectually appealing, the fallacy of such thinking was exposed more than 50 years ago by the philosopher-ecologist Garrett Hardin in a 1968 essay titled "The Tragedy of the Commons."[4]

The "commons" in Hardin's analysis describes a shared-resource system – such as a fishery – where individual entrepreneurs acting independently according to their own self-interest behave contrary to the common good of all stakeholders by depleting or spoiling that resource through their collective action. Consider, for example, the damage caused by high-tech trawlers used to harvest declining fish populations. By using more sophisticated technology, they achieve a short-term return on the fisherman's investment, but further deplete fish populations – a downward spiral that ends in tragedy for humanity, Nature and the future of fishing itself.

To redress this imbalance, both fish and their habitats must be considered stakeholders on a par with fishermen and consumers. This is not an easy thing for economists that esteem managing by results (MBR). But to Nordics grounded in the philosophy of folk Bildung, it is simply a matter of extending their "circles of belonging" from parochial concerns of their proximate business interests to more universal ones, such as the well-being of Nature and future generations. By approaching the living world through such a sense of mutuality and frugality, resource conservation becomes a matter of enlightened self-interest and personal responsibility.

This Nordic perspective also extends to finance, which in modern economies is an essential catalyst of innovation and progress. When finances are stable, people can think beyond themselves to the wellbeing of others, the planet and future generations – a process that bolsters symbiotic life-mimicking behavior. When finances are unstable, those without skills in systems thinking are apt to seek short-term quick fixes, including borrowing to cover costs of existing debt. Over the past two decades, that tendency has progressively weakened the debt-carrying capacity of the world economy and its largest borrowers (the US, China and Japan).

Nordic fiscal responsibility

Nordic countries approach borrowing the same way they do natural resources: with a frugal sense of limits. As a result, compared to their peers in the industrialized world, they have significantly less debt relative to GDP, higher savings rates, more secure social safety nets and better capitalized banks. Together, these attributes stabilize Nordic economies and support a wealth of human enterprise.

Instead of prioritizing quantities of GDP produced − a systems trap that has put the US and many other economies on a trajectory toward credit collapse − Nordic countries prioritize the quality of health, education and security available to their people. This places the emphasis where it belongs: because educated people are the primary means of their economic strength. Consequently, Nordic countries have some of the world's highest labor participation rates and per capita productivity − qualities that strengthen their economies and their capacities to continue investing in their people. Another dynamic feedback loop.

During the early 1990s, this pragmatic self-reinforcing approach was put to a severe test when Nordic governments and banks entered a short-lived financial crisis − the result of careless fiscal and lending practices that followed a period of financial deregulation. As mentioned in Chapter Three, rather than doubling down on failed policies that had been adopted to stimulate GDP, Nordic governments and banks, led by Sweden, pragmatically reformed their management practices.

Thanks to the speed and transparency with which Nordic governments implemented their fiscal and regulatory reforms, the crisis was quickly brought under control. From 1996 onward, the sovereign debt ratios of Nordic countries quickly improved, and the region's economic health was restored.

To understand the magnitude of Nordic fiscal reforms, the sovereign debt/GDP ratios of the three largest countries in 1993 ranged from 75% (Sweden) to the mid-50% range (Norway and Denmark). For purposes of comparison, US government debt at the time was roughly comparable at 65% of GDP.

Looking back on those reforms today, it is remarkable how effective Nordic countries were in changing the region's political-economic landscape. As revealed in Table 4.1, Nordic sovereign debt ratios today are

Table 4.1 Nordic sovereign debt ratios and credit ratings 2019

Country	Public Debt/GDP	Credit Rating
Denmark	33.2	AAA
Finland	59.4	AA+
Sweden	35.1	AAA
Norway	40.6	AAA
Iceland	37.0	A
Euro Area	84.1	–
USA	107.0	AA+

Sources: Trading Economics database (December 2019), Standard & Poor.

significantly lower than those of the US and the world's other advanced economies; and they would be even more favorable if the region's sovereign wealth funds were taken into consideration. While this is certainly due to the pragmatism and frugality of Nordic fiscal reforms, it also reflects the productivity of their people, who are generally healthier, better educated and often more motivated than their peers in the developed world.

These comparisons become more invidious when the US government's massive unfunded liabilities (implicit debt) are taken into consideration. For obvious reasons, Washington does not like to publicize such data, so it gets buried in obscure reports couched in opaque language that require a lot of detective work to discern. According to US Treasury data, the present value of unfunded liabilities to the government's social security system was $46.7 trillion for the fiscal year 2017 – a sum that was then roughly 2.5 times its then explicit credit market debt.[5]

Based on data provided in Appendix Four, the present value of such unfunded liabilities would likely exceed $60 trillion today (2020). However, according to the non-profit US Debt Clock, the actual federal unfunded liability would be more than double that amount once future commitments to Medicare and Medicaid are counted under more stringent actuarial assumptions.[6] Either way, total US government debt (explicit plus implicit) is considerably larger than reported.

Because Nordic pension and health care plans are fully funded, the large gap between US and Nordic sovereign debt ratios illustrated in Table 4.1 is much wider than shown. In light of these facts, Standard & Poor's AA+ credit rating for US government debt seems excessive. Were the US Federal

Reserve unable to print money to cover the US government's total debt, including unfunded liabilities, the nation's sovereign credit rating would be considerably lower.

Sovereign wealth funds and secure pensions

In making the foregoing comparisons, it is also worth noting that Nordic countries are more conservative in stating their sovereign debt ratios. At yearend 2019, Norway's $1.1 trillion sovereign wealth fund, for example, was worth more than 2.5 times the country's GDP ($402 billion). That means the country actually has substantially more liquid assets than debt.

Established in 1990 to save a portion of its offshore oil and gas revenues for pensioners and future generations, Norway's wealth fund clearly adds to the stability of its economy and universal safety nets. Further, by retaining a 67% share of Equinor, its giant energy company, the government of Norway sends an important message to its citizens: that their future well-being and security are more essential to the country than the transient wealth created for a privileged few by a depleting asset.

Iceland follows a similarly frugal policy. In 2016, its public and private pension assets represented 150% of its GDP – the fourth-highest funding ratio among the world's developed economies.[7] In addition, it too has created a sovereign wealth fund to offer future generations a protective buffer for contingencies. With a 2019 goal of 300 billion kroner ($2.5 billion), the equivalent to nearly 10% of its 2018 GDP ($26 billion), it has ample room to grow. Government contributions to the fund will be from dividend payments, rent and other revenues paid to its Treasury from the island's vast hydro, geothermal and wind power resources. Given Iceland's large foreign exchange reserves (roughly $6.4 billion at yearend 2019) and its substantial trade surplus, it has the resources to quickly fill its wealth fund.

Because pension funding is such an important criterion in assessing a country's credit-worthiness, it is worth noting that Nordic countries also have top ratings in the 2019 Melbourne Mercer Global Pension Index. Based on Mercer's scoring system, whose rankings are based on "funding adequacy, sustainability and integrity," The Netherlands was rated first with a score of 81, followed by Denmark (80.3), Australia (75.3), Finland (73.6), Sweden (72.3) and Norway (71.2). Had Iceland been included in Mercer's ratings, it would have held one of the world's top rankings, as indicated in the prior paragraph.[8]

To ensure the continuation of such prudent fiscal management, the finances of Nordic local governments are overseen by private companies in Denmark and Sweden (KommuneKredit, Kommuninvest) and by public/private consortia in Norway and Finland (Kommunalbanken, MuniFin). These oversight organizations bind local governments to policies of joint and several responsibility plus green circular economy practices. As a result of such prudence, Nordic communal bonds are among the world's top-rated "green bonds" with credit ratings ranging from Aa1/AA− (Finland) and Aaa/AAA (Denmark, Norway, Sweden).

Strong banks supported by high savings rates

In keeping with the frugality and financial strength of Nordic governments, the region's six leading banks, although small by global standards, are among the world's best capitalized and most efficient. Table 4.2 provides evidence of this in terms of 2019 credit ratings (first column); Tier 1

Table 4.2 Credit and Capital Ratios of Major Nordic Banks Compared to Top US and European Union Banks (2019)

Six Largest Nordic Banks	Credit Rating	Tier 1 Ratio	Expense Ratio
Danske Bank Group	A3/P2	17.3%	64.8%
DNB Bank*	Aa2/P1	18.3%	42.7%
Svenska Handelsbanken*	Aa2/P1	20.7%	48.8%
Nordea*	Aa3/P1	16.3%	57.0%
Swedbank*	Aa2/P1	19.4%	43.0%
Skandinaviska Enskilda Banken*	Aa2/P1	20.8%	46.0%
Largest US and EU Banks			
Bank of America	A2/P1	12.6%	60.2%
BNP Paribas*	Aa3/P1	12.1%	64.5%
Citigroup	A3/P2	13.0%	56.5%
Deutsche Bank	A3/P2	13.6%	NA
HSBC Holdings	A2/P1	14.7%	59.2%
JPMorgan Chase	A2/P1	14.2%	57.4%
Wells Fargo	A2/P1	12.8%	66.0%

Sources: Moody's plus 2019 bank annual reports.
*Banks rated by Global Finance Magazine as "the world's safest" in 2019 are marked with an asterisk (https://www.gfmag.com/magazine/november-2019/worlds-safest-banks-2019).
Deutsche Bank 2019 annual report did not disclose the foregoing ratios due to a €19.7 billion operating loss.

capital ratios, which reflect their financial strength (second column) and their efficiency ratios, which reveal operating expense relative to total income (third column).

By these standards, five of the six leading Nordic banks had top-tier credit ratings (Aa3/P1 or better) during 2019. By comparison, only one European bank met this standard (BNP). Notably, none of the big US banks were able to attain this high standard. The reason for this divergence becomes clear when we compare their Tier 1 ratios of core bank capital to risk-weighted assets. By this metric, the Nordic average for 2019 (18.80%) was more than 40% stronger than their largest US and European peers (13.28%).

Another key indicator of the financial strength of Nordic banks can be found in their low expense ratios – a measure of their operating efficiency. In this case, low ratios are preferable to high ones because they enable banks to maintain their capital strength. By this metric, the average operating expense ratios of the six largest Nordic banks (50.38%) was significantly lower than their US and European megabank peers. Even if we exclude Deutsche Bank, which had an operating loss of €5.7 billion in 2019, the average expense ratios of the remaining six (62.51%) suggest their cultures are more extravagant and risky. A likely reason for this gap in expense ratios is the fact that Nordic branch managers control most lending, which ensures that credit is allocated to locally known customers. In addition, Nordic banks do not indulge their executives with large bonuses, which reduces their temptation to take aggressive risks.

As a result of their frugal, cost-conscious cultures, five of the six Nordic banks listed in Table 4.2 were included in *Global Finance* magazine's 2019 list of the "World's safest banks." (Danske Bank, which was listed in the 2017 top 50, was demoted due to a self-reported 2018 money laundering case against its Estonian branch for which its CEO and board chair were fired.) In addition, three smaller Nordic banks were included on the 2019 top 50 list: Norway's Kommunalbanken, Sweden's Export Credit Bank and Finland's OP Corporate Bank. By contrast, none of the biggest US banks made the list.[9]

Another important component of the region's banking strength is the earlier mentioned Nordic Investment Bank (Chapter Two), which aims to serve the common good in support of the Nordic Council of Ministers' democratic ideal of a "sharing economy."[10] With a rare AAA/Aaa credit rating, it works in partnership with regional commercial banks – both in helping to evaluate risks and by co-lending with them. By focusing on the quality of lending, rather than the quantity of deals generated, the NIB has remained a preferred credit risk relative to major US investment banks, such as Morgan Stanley (A1) and Goldman Sachs (A3). The same holds true in comparisons with the giant US and European commercial banks shown in Table 4.1 – all of which engage in investment banking. Due to the aggressive risk-taking cultures of these megabanks, all but one (HSBC) had to be rescued at public expense following the 2008 global financial crisis; and all were later fined for malfeasance and corruption.[11]

We find further expressions of the Nordic region's frugality in its high gross national savings rates. Norway led in this metric with a huge savings rate of 36%, followed by Sweden and Denmark (29%), Finland (24%) and Iceland (21%) – all of which had higher 2019 savings rates than the US (19%).[12] In Nordic countries, the largest portion of such savings is held in government reserves that support citizens' health, education and retirement security. Were the US to adopt similar accounting methods, its savings rate would be negative due to its massive unfunded liabilities.

In addition to the substantial reserves set aside by Nordic governments, regional companies generally maintain strong reserves on their balance sheets – a quality that enables them to serve the public while doing cutting-edge research on renewable energy, bio-innovation and circular economy technologies. Because people working within such cultures feel secure and find meaning in what they do, they become more engaged and productive. Although this is not the stuff of economic texts, such operating leverage is real and largely explains why Nordic economies and companies have become global leaders in sustainable innovation and financial integrity.

World's most sustainable companies

Corporate Knights, a Canadian research company, publishes an annual list of the world's 100 most sustainable companies, which are presented each January at the World Economic Forum in Davos, Switzerland. Remarkably, 37 Nordic companies made the list over the decade ending in 2019. Of these, 27 were listed multiple times and 16 were included in the top 25 one or more times (as shown in Appendix Two). Notably, the 2020 list, which reflects prior year performance, gave Nordic companies the top three rankings. As earlier mentioned, this is an extraordinary achievement for a region with less than half of 1% of the world's population.

Criteria for selection in the Global 100 include financial stability, frugal management of energy, water and materials, employee safety, management diversity, quality of innovation and market capitalization ($2 billion minimum). Because of its comprehensive data-driven analyses, the Global 100 is one of the most widely respected sources on corporate sustainability and a barometer that investment companies avidly follow in framing their investment strategies.

One of the extraordinary shared attributes of Nordic companies named on the Global 100 list is their durability – an attribute grounded in their capacity to learn and adapt. Stora Enso is particularly interesting in this context because it has operated continuously since the 13th century – more than 700 years ago. As such, it is an outstanding example of Nordic frugality, adaptability and progressive thinking.

Regarded as one of the world's largest forest products companies, Stora launched a new strategic goal in 2006: to transform itself into a "renewable materials growth company" on the visionary premise that "everything made from fossil-based materials today can be made from a tree tomorrow." Today, with a rapidly growing percentage of sales in high value-added areas, such as biomaterials, biocomposites and high-end renewable packaging, more than 80% of its operating earnings before income tax (EBIT) are derived from such growth areas. To accelerate that trend, Stora screens and invests in startups that advance its vision; and in 2018, was awarded the title of Finland's most startup-friendly company. With a net debt/equity ratio of 32%, a plentiful free cash flow and substantial forest assets, it has the resources and commitment to advance its transformative mission.

If Stora Enso is the oldest company to be included in the Global 100, Atlas Copco is one of the most frequently mentioned. Founded in 1873, Atlas has made the list five times in the past decade. As a world leader in energy-efficient industrial tools and equipment, it serves corporate customers in 180 countries. One of its many innovations is a process for converting the energy used to power air compressors into heat-recovery systems, where up to 94% of the energy used to run the compressor is converted back into usable heat. Because compressed air is a common source of industrial power, this innovation offers customers rapid payback while also reducing the carbon emissions from heating fuels. Since steel represents 90% of raw materials used in production, Atlas Copco uses recycled steel in all products, thereby reducing costs and environmental impact. Given its skills in creating systems that save energy, materials and money, global demand for its products and services are robust. In 2019, Atlas Copco had a 35% return on equity (ROE) and a frugal net debt to equity ratio of only 23 percent.

As with Stora Enso and Atlas Copco, all Nordic companies named on the Global 100 list are renowned for their resource-efficient circular economy practices. Together, these have enabled them to grow sustainably with remarkably little debt.

This outcome contrasts with global trends in corporate borrowing, which often exceed the debt-carrying capacities of underlying borrowers. Reflecting this trend, *Barron's*, a weekly financial journal published by Dow Jones, cautioned in April 2019 that "Corporate credit ratings are falling at the fastest rate in years."[13] In November 2019, Moody's went a step further by issuing a downgrade warning on normally stable sovereign debt.[14]

Two months after that warning, the world awakened to the coronavirus pandemic. As national economies were forced into partial shutdowns to contain the virus, borrowers everywhere began to have difficulties servicing their debts. According to Fitch Ratings, by mid-May 2020, year-to-date defaults had reached a six-year high and were expected to quickly surpass their all-time high reached during the 2008 global financial crisis.[15] With major companies, like Ford, downgraded to junk bond status, the US government and the Federal Reserve were forced to undertake another round of corporate bailouts. Nordic companies, by contrast, were less harmed because of their strong balance sheets and strategic positioning in circular economy technologies. With more resources to fall back on, they were, in fact, advantageously positioned to gain market share in these emerging growth industries.

Qualities of Nordic sustainable leadership

One of the attributes of Nordic companies that enables them to operate with lower debt is their common focus on conserving energy, water and materials. Because such products and services enable others to do the same, global demand for their know-how generates consistently strong revenue and free cash flow. That enables them to maintain resilient balance sheets while investing aggressively in R&D – qualities that have generally kept them ahead of the curve in developing circular economy solutions.

Looking beyond traditional manufacturing, Nordic companies within the Global 100 offer a broad spectrum of energy and resource-saving services. Among these, four are worth mentioning for their diverse strategies: Storebrand, a leader in the fields of insurance and green investing; Ørsted, a pioneer in renewable energy systems; Novozymes, the global leader in enzyme technologies and Tomra, a technology frontrunner in recycling and resource recovery. As a seasoned group, all four contribute substantially to the region's economic growth and stability.

The oldest of these, Storebrand, also has a long history in the Nordic region. Founded in 1767, it has evolved from insurance and banking into green investing with a goal of "contributing to a sustainable transition" through "active ownership." In selecting portfolio investments, its analysts grade companies on their environmental, social and governance (ESG) policies with special attention given to carbon emissions and water consumption. Strategically, the company supports sustainable economic development by moving investment funds "from activities with a major negative impact on the climate to companies that are part of the transition to a greener economy." In doing so, Storebrand aims to create "a future our customers can look forward to" as well as securing its own future. As Norway's largest pension and mutual fund manager, Storebrand was an early mover (2013) in divesting fossil fuel companies that refused to aggressively diversify into renewable energy – a movement later joined by other global asset managers. In 2017, CEO Odd Arild Grefstad urged the Norwegian government to do the same – a policy adopted in 2019 by Norway's $1.1 trillion sovereign wealth fund. Because of Storebrand's reasoned incentive-driven approach, it earned second place in *Corporate Knights'* 2017 edition of the Global 100.

Ørsted is a company that actually made such a renewable energy transition. Formerly 100% owned by the Danish government – then operating as DONG Energy – it was for a long time the country's largest supplier of fossil fuel energy. Following successful ventures in developing renewable energy in Kalundborg plus offshore windfarms in Northern Europe, it sold roughly half its shares to investors in 2016 in order to gain greater access to world capital markets. Today, Ørsted is the world's largest developer of offshore windfarms with a strategic vision "to create a world that runs entirely on green energy." Aside from its technical expertise, Ørsted is a preferred partner in developing renewable energy systems thanks to its low net debt to equity ratio (16%) at yearend 2019 and its high operating margin of 17.4 percent.

Novozymes is another major contributor to the Nordic renewable energy revolution. As a world leader in bio-innovation, with a 48% market share in the fast-growing enzyme market, its technologies enable companies and municipalities to convert organic wastes into biofuels. In one of its first such projects (mentioned in Chapter One), it partnered with Ørsted in converting waste wheat straw into fuel for the Asnaes electric power station in Kalundborg. In addition, by creating biological solutions to replace petrochemicals in agriculture and industry, it helps customers cut costs, improve product quality and lower their ecological footprints. In agriculture, for example, its products enable farmers to grow more and better quality crops with fewer pesticides and fertilizers. Its enzyme solutions also help manufacturers save energy, chemicals and water while getting more value out of raw materials. According to Novozymes' 2019 annual report, its products helped customers avoid an estimated 87 million metric tons of carbon dioxide (CO_2) emissions during that year. With a low net debt ratio (19.8%), a strong return on equity (27.5%) and a high (11.0%) portion of revenue spent on research during 2019, the company remains at the leading edge of transformative innovation.

Tomra is the world's largest provider of resource recovery systems. With roughly 85,000 technologically-advanced recycling systems installed in 80 countries, its strategic vision is to "transform how we obtain, use and reuse resources for sustainable economic growth and improved quality of life for all." As the world leader in artificial intelligence (AI)-driven laser sorting technology, its recycling solutions are state-of-the-art. Considering the world's growing volumes of waste and the risks of disposing of these in waterways and landfills, Tomra is at the front of a global growth industry. Due to the speed and accuracy of its sensor technology, it has also created a growth market in food sorting and peeling – processes that cut waste and improve product quality for food retailers. With a moderate 2019 net debt ratio (49%) supported by strong free cash flow and a rapidly growing global customer base, Tomra exemplifies the Nordic region's culture of frugality, circular economy productivity and sustainable growth.

Although none of the companies mentioned in this chapter come to mind when we think of global growth leaders, they have generated excellent shareholder returns compared to commonly referenced indices of stock market returns, such as the Morgan Stanley Capital International (MSCI) World Index and the Standard & Poor (S&P) 500 Index.

For example, from the year 2000 (when Novozymes went public) to yearend 2019, its shares increased in value more than tenfold in local currency terms. Over the same time interval, the shares of Atlas Copco appreciated roughly twelvefold and those of Tomra nearly fourfold. Even allowing for currency fluctuations, these returns were substantially in excess of those on the S&P 500 and the MSCI World indices, which grew slightly more than twofold.

Stora Enso's share growth, although less compelling because it operates in what has long been a cyclical slow-growth industry, nevertheless significantly outperformed those of US giants International Paper and Weyerhaeuser. This was particularly true in the period since the global market crash of 2008/9, during which time it was in the early stages of its transformation into a renewable materials company. For the decade ending 2019, its shares nearly tripled in value while those of its US competitors either lost value (WY) or made modest gains (IP).

Storebrand's shares nearly tripled in value for the five years ending in 2019 following its pro-active approach to risk management adopted in 2013. In the brief time Ørsted shares traded between its initial public offering (IPO) in June 2016 and yearend 2019, its shares increased in value 168%, roughly triple that of the S&P 500.

Given such results, it is no wonder that green entrepreneurship is growing rapidly in the Nordic world. As Kalundborg and Nordic Global 100 companies demonstrate, circular economy solutions that use materials and energy more efficiently are less reliant on debt because they are less entropic (wasteful and disorderly) and more generative (inspiring, innovative). At a time when the US and world economies are virtually drowning in debt, these exemplars illuminate how and why Nordic economies have become global prosperity leaders.

Frugality as economic necessity

Considered in terms of energy and resource management, frugality explains how life on Earth has survived and thrived for 3.5–4 billion years. Its fundamental premise is simple. By keeping Earth's biological resources circulating in a symbiotic loop of mutually reinforcing nutrient exchanges, this process has generated a prodigious growth of species and intelligent life – all from the beginning of single-cell organisms. The extraordinary productivity of this loop resides in orderly and efficient (low entropy) exchanges of value wherein the health of the whole and those of its individual parts are indivisible.

Neoclassical economists have a hard time integrating this reality into their thinking because their models assume that people and their economies are super-species that transcend Nature and therefore operate by different rules. While this mental model was less harmful centuries ago when the world was sparsely populated and its biological resources seemed limitless, it is devastatingly ruinous today as population growth eats into Earth's dwindling reserves of natural resources.

The contrasts between neoclassical economic thinking and the organic (circular) processes of Nature are particularly evident in the realm of energy policy. Because the industrial revolution was launched on fossil fuels, neoclassical economists habitually assume that modern industrial economies must continue to prioritize them – in spite of the growing scarcity of such fuels and their damaging effects on human health, ecosystem degradation and climate change.

As Nordic economies are now showing us, this is unnecessarily wasteful because energy derived from Earth's renewable resources (sun, wind, biomass, hydro, geothermal) is today less expensive and healthier to the well-being of people and the biosphere, which together are the primary sources of all economic value.

As a symbol of enlightened Nordic frugality, renewable energy today plays a lead role in the region's economic ascendency and explains why Nordic countries have become more future-fit than the US and other fossil-fuel-centered economies. In addition to generating two-thirds of regional electricity from renewables (versus only 15% in the US), Nordic countries are also world leaders in the efficiency of their electricity distribution networks and in developing transportation fuels from biomass – subjects that will be addressed in future chapters.

A further Nordic advantage resides in their ethos of sufficiency as expressed in the Swedish proverb "*Lagom är bäst*," (translated: "the right amount is best"). Similar to natural systems, it conveys a sense of balance – an understanding that if *everyone has enough, communities will thrive*. As a widely-shared Nordic value, it is also a brake on the wastefulness of consumerism and planned obsolescence, which together have taken a heavy toll on Earth's biosphere.

Based on these facts, it is not surprising that Nordic countries are global prosperity leaders; that their debt ratios are significantly lower than those of the US and other industrial economies; that their leading banks are better capitalized and more efficient; that their social safety nets and pension funds are more secure; that their gross national savings rates are higher; and that they have a disproportionate share of the world's most sustainable corporations.

By embedding frugality as a core element of strategic thinking, Nordic countries seek to ensure there will be enough to go around in an over-populated, resource-stressed world. If you want to know why the Nordic Model works so well in comparison to the failing neoclassical one, frugality is a good place to start.

Notes

1 The Nordic Frugal Innovation Society. https://tnfis.org
2 Amy Yee. 2018. "In Sweden, trash heats homes, powers buses and fuels taxi fleets," *New York Times*. September 21, 2018. Available from: https://www.nytimes.com/2018/09/21/climate/sweden-garbage-used-for-fuel.html
3 For example, see: Sitra Launch Event. "LOOP circular economy ventures." December 5, 2018. https://www.sitra.fi/en/events/loop-circular-economy-ventures/
4 Garrett Hardin. 1968. "The tragedy of the commons," *Science Magazine*. 162(3859): pp. 1243–8. Available from: http://science.sciencemag.org/content/162/3859/1243 [Accessed June 29, 2020].
5 OASDI Trustees Report. 2017. https://www.ssa.gov/oact/tr/2017/VI_F_infinite.html#1000194. Table V.1.F.1
6 Truth in Accounting. 2019. "We've updated our debt clock." June 7, 2019. Available from: https://www.truthinaccounting.org/news/detail/weve-updated-our-debt-clock
7 The Icelandic Pension System. November, 2017. https://www.lifeyrismal.is/static/files/Fundargogn/2017pensions-in-iceland.pdf. p. 14.
8 Melbourne Mercer Global Pension Index. 2019. https://www.mercer.com.au/our-thinking/mmgpi.html
9 David Sanders. "The world's safest banks 2019," *Global Finance Magazine*. Available from: https://www.gfmag.com/magazine/november-2019/worlds-safest-banks-2019

10 Jon Erik Dølvik and Kristin Jesnes. 2017. "Nordic labor markets and the sharing economy," Nordic Council of Ministers.
11 Mike Collins. 2015. "The big bank bailout," *Forbes Magazine*. July 14. Available from: https://www.forbes.com/sites/mikecollins/2015/07/14/the-big-bank-bailout/#166c4d752d8 [Accessed June 29, 2020].
12 World Bank Open Data: Gross Savings (% of GDP). https://data.worldbank.org/indicator/NY.GNS.ICTR.ZS/
13 Alexandra Scaggs. 2019. "Corporate credit ratings are falling at the fastest rate in years. Investors should be worried," April 10. Available from: https://www.barrons.com/articles/corporate-credit-ratings-are-falling-at-the-fastest-rate-in-years-investors-should-be-worried-51554908506
14 Marc Jones. 2019. "Moodys cuts global sovereign rating outlook to negative for 2020," *Reuters*. November 13. Available from: https://www.reuters.com/article/global-ratings-moodys/moodys-cuts-global-sovereign-rating-outlook-to-negative-for-2020-idUSL8N27R3YG
15 Patturaja Murugaboopathy. 2020. "US leveraged loan results at six-year high as coronavirus hits business," *Reuters*. May 21. Available from: https://www.reuters.com/article/us-usa-debt-leveraged/u-s-leveraged-loan-defaults-at-six-year-high-as-coronavirus-hits-businesses-idUSKBN22X1BD

5

OPENNESS AS A LONG-TERM STRATEGY

Openness to change is a core aspect of the competitiveness of the Nordic economies.

Daniel Sachs, CEO Proventus AB[1]

The economic argument in favor of free trade and open markets is not that there are no losers, only that the winners have so much to gain that they can – in principle – compensate the losers.

ETLA and MIT[2]

Economies are living systems. Like Nature, they are constantly in flux as they process information, materials and energy within their environments. The more open they are to feedback from people and Nature (their primary assets), the more efficiently they operate.

Although logically appealing, maintaining an open economy is not as easy as it sounds because most business and political leaders think of economies as *closed systems* that operate by set (predictable) laws of supply and demand. Swayed by the theories of neoclassical economists, they believe economies are best managed by hierarchies who presumably understand the mechanics of the system. Under such regimes, anything that happens outside the bounds of their closed models – such as ecological degradation, climate change and related social stresses – is considered an "externality" that can eventually be fixed or overcome by human ingenuity.

This conceptual fallacy has launched most of today's industrial economies into a downward spiral of negative social, ecological and financial feedback. Further, because the life-mimicking Nordic Model and the mechanistic neoclassical model are such polar opposites, there is no middle ground. The only way to reverse the self-destructive tendencies of the neoclassical model is to convert to the more open life-mimicking one.

Such a cultural conversion can be done by peaceful democratic means, as Nordic countries have shown us, through voting and civic engagement. But it requires a high level of public awareness supported by education, a free press and complete transparency about political-economic activity.

Simply put, to live and work in harmony with the living world, we must adopt its open, life-affirming organization and methods. As proven methods, these draw us inexorably away from the closed deterministic thinking of the neoclassical paradigm and impel us to keep open minds as we learn and adapt within the ever-changing systems of Nature and our political economies.

To properly understand the complexities of our economies, we must first see them as they truly are: as sub-systems of life replete with infinite webs within webs ranging from single-cell bacteria to diverse ecosystems and complex human organizations.

When we think of economies in this context, we begin to realize that we can never manage them with mechanistic certainty. Overstressed living systems can break down quickly in ways few people understand at the time they happen. Incredibly, it was a simple bacterium (*Yersinia pestis*) that wiped out a third of Europe's population in the 14th century – an event that led to the breakdown of the feudal system and the emergence of the European Renaissance and Enlightenment. The bacterium that caused this plague was a byproduct of the filth and unhealthy living conditions of Europe's impoverished feudal underclass – a disruptor no-one understood until well after the fact.

Today's collapsing ecosystems and species extinctions are potentially more dangerous than the *Yersinia pestis* bacterium. As human populations grow and place higher demands (stresses) on Earth's biosystems, adverse biological consequences are increasing at unprecedented rates. Industrial impacts due to climate change and pollution already disrupt vital eco-systems with damaging effects to global food chains and human health. African swine fever, a highly contagious virus with no known cure and a near-zero survival rate, killed roughly half of China's pig herd between August 2018 and November 2019, and has now spread to neighboring countries (Mongolia, Russia, Cambodia, Laos, Vietnam). Although not contagious to humans, it disrupts a vital source of protein to China and Southeast Asia, which accounts for more than half of the world's pig population.

The ongoing COVID-19 virus is another powerful disrupter. First detected in China during November 2019, it is both highly contagious and lethal to humans. Within six months of its discovery, it had spread throughout the world, causing the full or partial closure of many companies, upset-ting global supply chains and forcing the onset of a global recession. The resulting contraction of global gross domestic product (GDP) and national incomes weighed most heavily on debt-leveraged countries, such as the US, China and Japan, which had to borrow additional trillions to manage the pandemic to which there is no end in sight.

As these biological upheavals accumulate along with ecosystem deg-radation, species extinction and climate change, the ecological and eco-nomic costs of continuing with the closed system thinking of neoclassical economics and business-as-usual have become ruinous. The impact on Nature's food chains and human food systems are already dire. Looking ahead to 2050, when the world's population will be higher by 2 billion (from 7.7 billion today to 9.7 billion), shifting to a more open, adaptive system will be less a matter of choice than one of survival.

> Environmental changes, including climate change, land degradation, water scarcity, and biodiversity loss – that are predicted to become more profound in the 21st century – pose significant challenges to global agri-culture, food security, and nutrition.
>
> US National Academy of Sciences, 2018[3]

Considered in this light, the open, adaptive Nordic Model presents a more sustainable way forward because it aims to harmonize means (healthy people and planet) with ends (a productive political-economic system) in ways that generate profit plus ecological and financial stability.

This is not to say that Nordic countries currently live within Earth's biological carrying capacity because their ecological footprints today are unsustainably high on a per capita basis. Nevertheless, they are the only advanced industrial region that has reduced its footprint since the 1970s when the world economy began its trajectory into ecological overstep (as shown in Appendix Three). Because a large part of the present Nordic footprint is due to the manufacture and transport of goods they import, the Nordic Council of Ministers and regional companies have placed high priorities on greening their supply chains and helping to advance the UN's 2030 Sustainable Development Goals. By such means, they intend to expand the reach of their life-mimicking model by drawing others into it − a multiple win proposition for themselves, the world economy and future generations.

When cultures shift to this more holistic way of thinking, people begin to understand the links between themselves, their economies and the complex, multi-layered web in which they exist, and they begin to take personal responsibility for improving the quality of life wherever they can. That awakening is transformative whenever it occurs because it shifts people from narrow ego-centric to more open spiritual eco-centric ways of thinking, exemplified by the student leaders of Helsinki's Slush movement.

A critical attribute of democracy

Such openness works best in democratic societies where information can be freely exchanged through an independent press and uninhibited political dialogue. Rather than being chaotic and disorderly, as leaders in hierarchical cultures avow, open, egalitarian democracies are in fact the most stable and effective form of organization. Because they engage diverse minds in problem solving rather than a select few (too often corrupt) individuals at the top, they are more adept at systems thinking and creative problem solving.

That is why Nordic countries achieve top standings in the Economist Intelligence Unit's global Democracy Index as well as world indices related to freedom, education, human health, prosperity, quality of life and happiness. It also clarifies why the US and countries with more closed hierarchical systems are falling behind on these very measures.

If we think of these links as we do the open feedback systems of Nature, we find a series of mutually reinforcing loops: where open democratic access to education and information enables people to make good political-economic decisions; where those decisions feedback to strengthen the social and governance systems on which they depend and where that very strength keeps the cycle going in a healthy, self-reinforcing way.

Such openness must, of course, embrace negative as well as positive feedback because such reminders force us to think in more integrated ways. When free-thinking people encounter failure or resistance, for example, they begin to question their assumptions (described in Chapter Three as double-loop learning). If that fails to yield understanding, many go on to explore possibilities outside their normal framework of thinking (triple-loop learning). Given the holistic nature of Nordic education, such higher levels of thinking and learning are more natural to Scandinavian people than to those who live in closed political-economic cultures.

In open political-economic cultures, the value of negative feedback cannot be overstated because it tells us when systems are stressed and getting out of balance. By freely inviting such feedback, democratic countries can step back and reflect on the adverse consequences of their behavior and adjust accordingly.

Closed cultures, by contrast, too often dismiss and override such inconvenient danger signals by treating symptoms rather than causes. Since the turn of the millennium, such remedies in the US have relied more and more on increasing the money supply, lowering interest rates, diluting accounting regulations, weakening antitrust laws and hedging with derivative financial instruments – none of which address the core issues of ecological, economic and social distress. By so doing, these interventions actually make adverse situations worse by covering up risk and blinding people to the perilous conditions they are creating.

The fallacy of such solutions was powerfully exposed by the value at risk (VAR) models that nearly blew up the global financial system in 2008. Rather than addressing the core problem of unsustainable debt growth that threatened the US and world economies at the time, these models supported a complex web of derivatives hedging that made those problems seemingly disappear. The objective was to reassure markets and increase the volume of lending and spending, which bankers and their regulators hoped would drive GDP and spending higher, thus enabling the system to heal itself.

Later, when defaults on such risky lending began to threaten bank capital, the banks at the center of this scheme packaged their loans into "collateralized" mortgage and debt obligations, which they in turn sold to the public as low-risk investments. This enabled them to clean up their balance sheets and continue writing new loans. But it made the underlying problem worse by shifting the burden to other parts of the global financial market, including public pension funds and insurance companies.

Eventually, the failures of hyper-leveraged mortgage and credit card borrowers became a tidal wave, which upset the stability of the interconnected global financial system. As credit markets seized up in 2008, the banks at the center of this fraudulent merry-go-round were pushed to the edge of failure. To avoid such a collapse, the most egregious ones – primarily money center banks in New York – were bailed out at the public expense and allowed to cover up their remaining shaky loans via changed accounting standards. To make matters worse, regulators permitted these banks to pay near-record bonuses to their executives in 2008 as if nothing amiss had happened.

Although the worst offending banks later faced multi-billion dollar fines for their fraudulent behavior, these were mitigated by the US Federal Reserve, which made credit available to them at near-zero cost. In addition, to increase the flow of new credit into the US economy, the Federal Reserve purchased trillions in US government bonds and mortgages, thereby re-liquefying markets and driving interest rates to near-zero (artificial) levels – policies it hoped would lift stock and bond prices enough to stimulate further GDP growth.

In short, instead of learning from negative feedback around the 2008 financial crisis (and prior crises of speculative excess), the US government and Federal Reserve continued to artificially support the economy. Driven by their equally determined efforts to boost GDP and remain competitive in world commerce, the European Union, Japan and China also continued to lend money at near-zero interest rates. Collectively, these reactions became another tragedy of the commons, because they drove the world economy deeper and deeper into debt relative to GDP – creating a financial burden that would last for generations.

Compared to the closed system solutions of these global economic powers, Nordic countries have openly and democratically addressed the core issues of ecological, social and financial stress that challenge modern economies. In doing so, they have invested aggressively in renewable energy and circular economy technologies while reducing the amount of sovereign debt they carry relative to GDP – activities that have also strengthened their universal safety nets.

This is not to say the path to Nordic learning has been easy. The tenfold rise in oil prices during the 1970s and their home-grown financial crisis of the early 1990s were both shocks to their political economies. As learning experiences, however, they galvanized the Nordic community's capacity for pragmatic systems thinking and multiple-loop learning, nudging them toward the life-mimicking cultures they are today.

The secret to their skills in such learning, as described in Chapter Three, resides in their philosophy of education (*Bildung*) and their open democratic systems, which enable Nordic people to see and adapt to the world "as it is" rather than trying to manage and control it by artificial means.

Openness as the Nordic way

One of the most frequently heard criticisms about Nordic economies is the high cost of taxes on individual incomes, carbon and consumption. When presented in a closed system framework, this sounds unreasonable and counter-productive. But when considered in a more open, holistic context, such taxes are in fact productive because they discourage wastefulness while the revenues they generate strengthen the safety nets that stabilize their economies. Further, by supporting public health, education and welfare, Nordic tax systems remove these burdens from companies – enabling them to focus more purposefully on their creative capabilities.

Considered as a whole, Nordic tax systems support the region's egalitarian, democratic culture and capacity for sustainable growth. When levied on personal incomes, they return fair value in services rendered and social stability. When levied on commercial added value (with exemptions for necessities, such as health care), they encourage frugal household and corporate budgeting. When levied on activities that pose ecological risks, they limit risky behaviors. In sum, they nudge countries in directions that strengthen people and Nature, whose wellbeing is critical to economic value creation and progress.

To Nordic high earners, high individual income tax rates are perceived as a reasonable price to pay for the culture of trust that simplifies commercial life. In addition, they enable Nordic countries to offer relatively low tax rates to companies whose financial well-being is essential to the region's prosperity. For purposes of comparison, regional corporate tax rates – 24% in Norway, 22% in Denmark and Sweden and 20% in Finland and Iceland – are competitive with the unified US corporate tax rate (federal and state) of 24% and with a globally-weighted average tax rate of 29.8 percent.

The openness of Nordic economies is also supported by local laws, which assure entrepreneurs and business leaders that they will receive fair treatment – an assurance that makes them feel freer to invest and innovate. According to the World Justice Project, Nordic countries were the top performers in its 2019 Rule of Law Index. Out of 113 countries evaluated, Denmark was rated first, Norway second, Finland third and Sweden fourth – a repeat of their prior-year rankings. The US, by comparison, was rated 20th, a downgrade from its prior position. Iceland was not rated in the Index due to its small size.[4]

The credibility of the Rule of Law Index is supported by the high standings of Nordic countries (relative to the US) in previously-mentioned global surveys on the quality of democracies, freedom from corruption, transparency and social progress – all of which support business and economic development.

The openness of Nordic economies is further enhanced by their commitments to free trade. Because their markets are small, they rely heavily on exports to achieve economies of scale and stay globally competitive. Consequently, instead of creating trade barriers to protect local businesses – policies that could compromise their free trade credentials – they look to what the world needs, particularly in terms of sustainable technologies, goods and services.

In sum, the open ideals of Nordic democracies – expressed in their tax systems, laws and free trade principles – contributes mightily to their economic well-being. We see strong evidence of this in Table 5.1, which lists countries in order of their standing in *The Economist*'s Intelligence Unit's Democratic Health Index, and shows how these, in turn, correlate with social progress, productivity, prosperity and sustainability – areas where Nordic countries have regularly been in the global vanguard.

In reviewing the foregoing five categories shown over time, it is interesting to note how consistently Nordic countries attain top ten or nearby rankings. The only apparent inconsistency is Norway's rating for productivity

Table 5.1 Where sustainability thrives

Country	Democracy[a]	Social Progress[b]	Productivity[c]	Prosperity[d]	Sustainability[e]
Norway	1	1	19	2	6
Iceland	2	6	5	10	3
Sweden	3	5	3	4	1
New Zealand	4	7	16	7	12
Denmark	5	2	8	1	4
Canada	6	9	18	19	19
Ireland	7	14	10	12	14
Finland	8	4	7	5	2
Australia	9	12	20	17	42
Switzerland	10	3	1	3	5
Netherlands	11	11	2	6	29
Luxembourg	12	8	15	9	8
Germany	13	8	9	8	15
UK	14	13	4	11	11
USA	25	26	6	19	34

Approximately 195 countries were rated in each of these surveys. Top ten ratings are rare. Nordic countries are rated in the top decile in all categories where ratings are available.

[a] Economist Intelligence Unit, 2019 Democratic Health Index. https://currentaffairs.gktoday.com/democracy-index-2019-key-facts-01201964364.html

[b] Social Progress Imperative. 2019 Social Progress Index. https://www2.deloitte.com/global/en/pages/about-deloitte/articles/social-progress-index-results.html

[c] CMC Global. 2019 Global Rankings of Innovation, Productivity & Quality Competitiveness. https://www.cmc-global.org/content/global-rankings-innovation-productivity-quality-competitiveness

[d] Legatum Prosperity Index 2019. https://www.prosperity.com/rankings

[e] Solability. The Global Sustainable Competitiveness Index 2019.

(19) by the International Council of Management Consulting Institutes (CMC). Although respectable, this was below OECD data on GDP per hour worked, where Norway is normally rated in the top three.[5] It also comes in below Norway's ranking in the 2019 Sustainable Competitive Index.

The most notable divergence in Table 5.1, however, is how the US, once a global prosperity leader, is falling behind in categories where it once led. Now rated a "flawed democracy," it was rated 25th in the 2019 Democracy Index (down from 17th in 2006). Likewise, in the Social Progress Imperatives Index, its rating has dropped to 26th (down from 16th in 2014). In fact, the one area where it achieved a top ten rating (productivity) is now questionable due to the large amount of debt it has used to advance GDP. According to a 2019 analysis published by Bloomberg, when adjusted for net debt, US productivity actually rates near the bottom.[6]

Commenting on the differences between the closed system US approach and the open system Nordic Model, Daniel Sachs, CEO of the

Swedish investment company Proventus Capital, observes that in spite of "shared beliefs in democracy and openness to change … [Americans and Scandinavians] go about it precisely in the opposite manner." Instead of trying to minimize individual taxation for the benefit of powerful elites, as the US does, Nordic "haves" share their personal gains with those who are less fortunate and more vulnerable through taxes that finance comprehensive social benefits. These, in turn, stabilize the system and support productivity by raising the value of human capital available to local companies.

Sachs says,

> [A]s a businessman, I like the Nordic Model (because its) high levels of trust, fairness and transparency also mean that transaction costs are low. Corruption is low. Agreements can be kept short and relatively uncomplicated, information about the people one is dealing with is abundant in the public domain, and the powerful and wealthy are closely scrutinized by the media. By contrast, transaction costs are high in the U.S. system.[7]

Embracing globalization and sharing risks

The magic of the Nordic Model, as Sachs asserts, resides in attending to the health of the whole by supporting its most vulnerable parts. In doing so, its universal safety nets have a dual role: first, by stabilizing local economies during disruptive economic events so people can carry on with their lives and feed their families as they adjust to new circumstances, and second, as an ongoing investment in the region's human capital and productivity.

A consortium of Nordic economists, writing for the Research Institute for the Finnish Economy (ETLA) and MIT, distil this holistic approach into five words: "Embracing Globalization and Sharing Risks."[8] The first two words describe Nordic willingness to compete in world markets, based on the quality, ingenuity and productivity of their people. The last two explain how they do so by sharing the costs of social overhead (e.g., investing in their people) plus relieving the financial stress of disruptive economic events.

The Nordic region's speedy recovery from the global financial crisis of 2008/9 illustrates the effectiveness of this strategy. Because their safety nets cushioned the financial shock, the region was able to continue building on its competitive advantages in renewable energy and circular economy technologies with a minimum of disturbance. Only Iceland, which had a banking crisis of its own, was disrupted; yet unlike the US, the bankers whose recklessness caused this crisis, instead of getting bonuses, went to jail. Thanks to such integrity, Iceland too recovered quickly and today has one of the world's highest rates of per capita GDP.

The synergies of this mutually reinforcing system are wonderful examples of Nordic pragmatism. As a system of risk management, the Nordic Model enables workplaces to adjust if global disorders or competition force them to close down or restructure. Companies can lay off workers without meeting union resistance because government flexicurity programs are available to support workers while they train for new opportunities. This in turn enables Nordic countries to reallocate workers and resources into more competitive growth areas – thereby increasing their economic efficiency, terms of trade and export potential. In circular fashion, the benefits of such strengthening keep Nordic economies healthy and able to support their safety nets.

Reinforcing this positive loop of risk sharing and economic adaptation is a sense of public trust in the ways Nordic governments manage their universal care programs. This reassures citizens that they are secure and that the money they pay out in taxes is well spent.

Consider, for example, the efficiency of Nordic health care systems. In 2016 the annual per capita health care costs in Finland ($4,033) and Iceland ($4,376) were less than half those in the US ($9,892), while those in Denmark ($5,205), Sweden ($5,488) and Norway ($6,647) were well below the US average.[9] In spite of such lower costs, Nordic people have longer life expectancies at birth – ranging from 71.7 years (Finland) to 73 years (Iceland and Norway) compared to 68.5 (USA).[10]

Nordic school systems also provide world-class service at a modest cost. Their schools are rated among the world's best in terms of early-childhood enrollment rates, academic proficiency, skill development and graduation rates from high school and college. As revealed in Chapter Three, 93% of Finns graduate from academic or vocational high schools (17.5 percentage points higher than the United States) and 66% go on to higher education, the highest rate in the European Union. Yet Finland spends about 30% less per student than the US.

The efficiency of governments in managing these programs strengthens Nordic economies by making their people more productive in terms of per capita GDP and by investing them with a desire to contribute, which is evident in their high labor participation rates (described below). These two attributes in turn strengthen social safety nets by virtue of the taxable incomes they generate – creating a reinforcing loop that keeps economies running at or near their full capacities.

The high labor participation rates of Nordic countries (defined as the percentage of their working-age populations who are employed) is an important part of this reinforcing cycle of positive economic feedbacks. According to 2019 surveys by Trading Economics, a global data firm, Nordic countries have some of the industrial world's highest labor participation rates with Iceland at 82.0%, Sweden 72.7%, Norway 71.3%, Denmark 69.9% and Finland 66.0% – all five of which perform above the US at 63.2 percent.[11] This is largely due to the structure of universal care plans, which provide health and education benefits to all plus generous time off for parents to provide child care. According to Norway's Ministry of Finance, working mothers today add to the country's net national wealth – a value equivalent to its total petroleum wealth.

Adding to this productivity advantage is the number of citizens who choose to work beyond their normal retirement ages. Because Nordic citizens are healthy and educated, many continue working as a means of fulfillment. Understanding the value of their contributions, Nordic governments extend the times when citizens can pay into their pension plans with accompanying tax benefits. According to Norway's 2011 pension reform law, citizens can work up to the age of 75, during which time they can contribute to "pension entitlements" on a tax-favored basis. In Sweden, people who work beyond the age of 65 are given a job tax reduction while they also collect comfortable retirement benefits. The same is true in Finland, where post-retirement pension contributions are exempt from municipal taxation. With such incentives, the ratio of people who work beyond retirement age is significantly higher in these countries than in most industrial (OECD) nations; and given the high education standards of Nordic people, demand for their services is robust.

Taken together, the high percentage of Nordic people engaged in productive work strengthens the region's capacity to thrive in a competitive world, as suggested in the foregoing ETLA/MIT article on "Embracing globalization and sharing risks." Like healthy ecosystems, the more open and symbiotic they are in developing the health of the whole, the more adaptive and regenerative they become.

This strategy, as shown throughout this book, works better than the more closed, mechanistic approach of the US and industrial economies that manage by results (MBR). By placing a higher value on the means of their prosperity (people and Nature) than on the end results of GDP and profit, Nordic economies elevate their potential for both systemic health and sustainable prosperity.

Countries holding on to the neoclassical model of industrial capitalism in the meantime have become trapped in a negative cycle of ecological and financial overreach, which depletes both human and natural resources. Like the US, the more they borrow to keep their dysfunctional economies afloat, the more destabilized they become as the costs of debt service out-run GDP (as indicated in Appendix Four).

This is not to suggest that Nordic economies are invulnerable. Similar to all developed economies, they are today challenged by demographically aging populations. With fewer working-age people entering the workforce to support a growing cohort of retirees, the region's universal safety nets are exposed.

To mitigate this bottleneck and relieve regional labor shortages, Nordic countries have opened themselves to immigrant refugees from war-torn countries in the Middle East and Africa. Although critics of such a policy fear it will create culture clash and friction, Nordic countries have gener-ally had a good experience with integrating people from different cultures into their midst.

Immigration as a solution

Because Nordic economies have been growing sustainably, they have been able to absorb large numbers of migrants. During the period of peak refu-gee migration into Nordic countries (2015/16), Sweden, which took the largest number of refugees, had average GDP growth of nearly 4% – roughly double that of the US and European Union.

Because most incoming migrants were families whose adult members came with skills, local organizations quickly coalesced to help them find work. One of the most effective was Sweden's Snabbspåret: a fast-track to employment program that matches the skills and experience of new arriv-als with jobs in schools and industries that were facing worker shortages. Tracks included Swedish language coaching and on-the-job training with a mentor and guidance counselor. Given the strength of Sweden's economy, local companies and organizations participated eagerly. Among the services offered, some Swedish startups offered apps to connect skilled migrants with employers and other resources.

To accommodate refugees with university educations and professional backgrounds, Swedish universities created programs to bring their home country credentials into compliance with local standards. Among these, the University of Gothenburg, in co-operation with the Swedish Council for Higher Education and other universities, offers a supplementary study program that gives higher education credits toward obtaining licenses needed to work within various professions. In addition, the Stockholm School of Economics offers migrants with a business background a ten-week mini-MBA in management studies and Swedish work culture followed by seven-month internships at select Swedish companies and banks; and the Royal Institute of Technology offers a software development academy with a three-month Java coding program for those with technical backgrounds.

This is not to say that assimilating refugees in Sweden has been an easy process – especially in situations where unaccompanied minors became engaged in criminal activities. Nevertheless, with the exception of a few incidents that drew global attention because of their infrequency, crime rates in Sweden have been moderate and well below those of the US. This is especially true in the more serious offenses of robbery, assault and homicide.[12] As a result, centrist pro-immigrant coalitions collected roughly 80% of the vote in Sweden's September 2018 general election while the anti-immigrant Sweden Democrats won less than 18 percent.

> Sweden's rapid intake of huge numbers of refugees and migrants, about 600,000 in total over the past five years, has produced some of the highest growth rates in Europe and will also help it address the challenges of an otherwise aging population... Foreign-born workers accounted for all the job growth in the industrial sector last year and for 90 percent of the new jobs in the welfare sector, in particular health care and elderly care.
>
> Bloomberg, 2018[13]

As a matter of historic record, Sweden's openness to refugees reflects positive long-term experience. According to the Nordic Council of Ministers, the labor participation rates for immigrant men and women increase steadily as they become integrated into the economy so that "after 20 years (based on those who arrived in 1997), there is barely any difference in the employment rate for females (69.3%) and males (69.6%)."[14] Such high labor participation rates are well above the 2018 IMF world average (61.4%), indicating that they add to Sweden's economic activity while symbiotically strengthening its social safety nets.

Nordic success in assimilating refugee migrants is further supported by the results of the 2018 World Happiness Report, which included a happiness sub-index for 117 countries with significant immigrant populations. In this survey, immigrant happiness in Nordic countries was remarkably close to those of native Scandinavians. In this sub-index, immigrants in Finland were happiest, followed by Denmark (2), Norway (3), and Sweden (7).[15] This affirms efforts to include immigrants in the culture and benefits of those countries – a result that has enabled them to join the economic mainstream quickly. (Iceland was not rated on this sub-index because it had too few immigrants.)

Since the migration peak of 2015/16, Nordic governments have tightened their admission standards for immigrants to ease the burden on regional welfare systems and to assimilate refugees already admitted. While these policies have slowed admissions, Nordic countries nevertheless remain remarkably open to immigration because the economic benefits have so far outweighed the risks.

Attending to the *real* real world

Open systems have a critical advantage over closed ones. By attending to economies as they really are – as sub-systems of life rather than imagined super-systems that are above life – Nordic economies gain immediate benefits. Just as life on Earth has been able to adapt and flourish for billions of years, countries that model their economies on Nature's open, egalitarian (democratic) processes have become more adaptive and prosperous, as revealed in Table 5.1.

As we look more deeply into the Nordic Model in Chapter Six, we will see how such openness invites the development of symbiotic relationships that coordinate and strengthen economic activity. These catalyze a huge evolutionary step forward because they generate co-operation and harmony rather than endless struggles for economic advantage and control, which are presently destroying capitalism from within. Although neoclassical economists tend to dismiss such motivations as fuzzy and elusive, it is hard to dismiss the results.

Notes

1 Daniel Sachs. 2012. "The Nordic model's economic appeal," *The Globalist.* May 28. Washington, DC. Available from: https://www.theglobalist.com/the-nordic-models-economic-appeal/ [Accessed June 29, 2020].

2 Torben Andersen et al. 2017. *The Nordic Model: Embracing Globalization and Sharing Risks.* ETLA B, The Research Institute of the Finish Economy, number 232. p. 18. Available from: https://economics.mit.edu/files/5726 [Accessed June 29, 2020].

3 Pauline Scheelbeek et al. 2018. "Effect of environmental changes on vegetable and legume yields and nutritional qualit," *Proceedings of the National Academy of Sciences of the USA.* Available from: https://www.pnas.org/content/115/26/6804

4 World Justice Project. *Rule of Law Index 2019.* Available from: https://worldjusticeproject.org/our-work/publications/rule-law-index-reports/wjp-rule-law-index-2019#:~:text=The%20World%20Justice%20Project%20Rule%20of%20Law%20Index%C2%AE,Security%2C%20Regulatory%20Enforcement%2C%20Civil%20Justice%2C%20and%20Criminal%20Justice.

5 Niall McCarthy. 2019. "Where labor productivity is highest," *Statista.* May 27. Available from: https://www.statista.com/chart/16905/gdp-per-hour-worked-across-the-total-economy/

6 Vincent Del Giudice et al. 2019. "America's wealth hinges on its ability to borrow big – or else," *Barrons.* August 31. Available from: https://www.bloomberg.com/news/articles/2019-08-31/america-s-wealth-hinges-on-its-ability-to-borrow-big-or-else

7 Op. Cit. Sachs. "The Nordic model's economic appeal."

8 Torben M Andersen et al. "The Nordic model," (Helsinki 2007): https://economics.mit.edu/files/5726

9 For 2016 OECD data on health care spending, see: https://data.oecd.org/healthres/health-spending.htm

10 World Health Organization. 2016. "Healthy life expectancy (HALE) data by country." Available from: http://apps.who.int/gho/data/node.main.HALE?lang=en

11 Trading Economics. 2019. "Labor force participation rate," https://tradingeconomics.com/country-list/labor-force-participation-rate

12 Martin Schori. 2019. "The crime situation in Sweden compared to the US, in 4 charts," *Aftonbladet.* July 26. Available from: https://www.aftonbladet.se/nyheter/a/WP0KG/the-crime-situation-in-sweden-compared-to-the-us-in-4-charts

13 Rafaela Lindeberg. 2018. "Sweden's economy is getting a lift from migrants," *Bloomberg Businessweek.* August 21. Available from: https://www.bloomberg.com/news/articles/2018-08-21/sweden-s-economy-is-getting-a-lift-from-migrants

14 Nordic Council of Ministers. 2018. *State of the Nordic Region Immigration and Integration Edition*, p. 61. Available from: https://norden.diva-portal.org/smash/get/diva2:1192284/FULLTEXT01.pdf [Accessed June 29, 2020].

15 World Happiness Report 2018. Based on pooled results from Gallup World Poll Surveys from 2015–2017. http://worldhappiness.report/ed/2018/

6

THE VALUE OF SYMBIOTIC VISION

Vision is the most vital step in the policy process.

Donella Meadows[1]

The transformation to a bio-based economy means a transition from a fossil fuel-based economy to a more resource-efficient economy based on renewable materials produced through sustainable use of ecosystem services from land and water. A greater focus on research and innovation can provide us with new products developed from biomass that will replace fossil material, combat climate change, reduce waste and create new jobs.

The Nordic Bioeconomy Initiative, 2019[2]

The word "symbiosis" is an amalgam of two Greek words meaning "living" and "together." As used today, it most commonly refers to relationships that yield mutual advantages to different species living in relationship with one another. This is a particularly apt descriptor of Nordic culture, where symbiotic principles are embedded in their egalitarian model of democracy, their universal care systems and their shared goals of sustainable development.

Philosophically, these principles implicitly recognize that living assets (people and Nature) are the source of all value creation. As a defining attribute of Nordic civilization, this worldview moves people to live and work harmoniously with Nature and each other, to be frugal in their use of resources and open-minded to transformative ideas that challenge status quo thinking. Later in this chapter, we will see how such ideals have enabled Nordic companies operating in traditional, slow-growth industries (forest products, farming, electricity generation and food processing) to reinvent their businesses in dynamic new ways.

Before exploring these stories, however, it is important to understand the importance Nordic people assign to symbiotic thinking. Of the six life-mimicking attributes described in Chapter One, this is the quality that most arouses their passions to think creatively and innovate. From the early circular economy experiments in Kalundborg to the ardent outpourings of Helsinki's annual Slush events, symbiotic thinking has become a unifying theme – a way of seeking new paths in a world challenged by ecosystem degradation, climate change, poverty and disease.

The Nordic Bioeconomy Initiative (NordBio) is a wonderful example of this. Initiated by the Nordic Council of Ministers in 2013, its stated goal was to "encourage a proactive response to climate change, open new markets, create new jobs, contribute to food security and public health, and secure access to bio-based feedstock in the Nordic countries and beyond."

Strategically, NordBio sought to replace ecologically damaging fossil fuels, and their toxic chemical derivatives, with bio-based alternatives derived from regional forests, farmland, fisheries, marine plants and microorganisms. Noting that roughly a third of such biomass is commonly discarded as useless waste, the initiative's idea was to use these residues as feedstock for biofuels, biochemicals and bioplastics – goods that enable the creation of multiple higher value products.

To do this, NordBio proposed to develop a network of biorefineries, operating as Nordic test centers for green energy solutions that would create energy and useful materials from regional sources of biomass. For example, blue biorefineries would focus on marine biomass, including fish waste and discard macroalgae; green biorefineries would process green grass and other green plant materials; yellow biorefineries would harvest yellow biomass, straw, stover and wood; gray biorefineries would convert food processing waste; brown biorefineries would create value from sludge and waste water treatment and others would process household waste as feedstock. By using green (biological) methods to convert such waste into new products, these refineries would symbiotically encourage the protection of the region's biological resources, which provide vital ecosystem services such as carbon capture, improved wildlife habitat, clean air and fresh water.

Contemporaneous with NordBio's launch in 2013, the BIOPRO Academy and World Campus was opened in Kalundborg. As mentioned in Chapter One, this symbiotic collaboration, funded by the Novo Nordisk Foundation, includes companies pragmatically engaged in the Kalundborg Symbiosis plus the University of Copenhagen and the Danish Technical University (DTU). Created to find new approaches to production that would optimize the Nordic region's vast biological resources (oceans, forests, farms), it embodied NordBio's larger ideals to advance education and economic development.

One of the most interesting technologies to emerge from these collaborations was the development of specialized cell cultures called "cell factories" capable of producing high-value biopharmaceuticals, anti-infective compounds, industrial chemicals, fine and specialty chemicals and nutritional supplements from regional bioresources – all multi-billion-dollar industries with significant growth potential.

In addition to creating new products from locally available biomaterials, Nordic companies inspired by NordBio have developed advanced technologies that enable them to partner with Nature rather than trying to control and dominate it. By adapting digital technologies (artificial intelligence, nanotechnology) to their symbiotic goals, they have been able to increase the value of regional biological resources and in so doing, create whole new industries.

In the circular bioeconomy, biological materials can be upgraded and reused in many types of new value chains to obtain more primary products from the raw materials. Complex molecules such as proteins from industrial side-streams and household waste can be recovered as building blocks for new microbial products, as advanced biofuels, biomaterials and biochemicals, and by recycling nutrients back to the soil. What remains after all usable elements have been utilized can be converted through combustion into electricity and heat (bioenergy recovery).

Danish Technical University, 2015[3]

In keeping with the Nordic region's holistic philosophy of education (Bildung), NordBio was organized to advance education *at all levels*. Beyond increasing regional productivity, it aimed to

> make research and academic work in the fields of sustainable pro-duction and utilization more attractive to future generations; bring together science, technology, education and culture at various school levels, in institutions and the economy; and offer a joint Nordic venue and platform for co-operation, collaboration and exchange of views across ages and fields of expertise.[4]

In this sense, it sought to deepen the cultural affiliation Nordic people feel toward their natural environment – both as a good in its own right and as an investment in the future.

In the following sections, we will look at four Nordic companies that have reinvented basic slow-growth industries in ways that create new rev-enue streams. Each company launched new symbiotic strategies the year NordBio was initiated (2013) or shortly thereafter. Together, their stories reflect the region's upward spiral of wealth-creating enterprise that have strengthened local economies and capital markets.

Similar to most Nordic innovation leaders, all four companies framed their strategies as symbiotic ideals, including the UN's Sustainable Development Goals. By so expanding their corporate missions (circles of belonging), they inspired employees to work with their hearts as well as their minds – an appeal to their highest spiritual intelligence (SQ). Perhaps more than any other factor, this explains why Nordic countries continually lead in the field of sustainable economic development.

Reinventing the forest industry

In 2013, Finland's UPM-Kymenne reinvented itself as the "Biofore Company." The name was intended to convey a new strategic vision of using biotechnologies to transform the forest industry into a source of "high quality alternatives to non-renewable materials, both profitably and responsibly." To advance its vision, UPM developed the world's first com-mercial-scale refinery to produce biofuels, bioplastics and biopharmaceu-ticals from sustainable forest resources. The success of this transformation is reflected in the price of its stock, which more than tripled in value in the seven years since Biofore was launched (2013–2019) – a time when the shares of US forest products giants International Paper and Weyerhaeuser stood still or lost value.

Prior to reinventing itself, UPM shares traded in parallel with other companies in the cyclical forest products industry, including its US peers. Consequently, it is fair to say that the Biofore strategy made a significant difference to its value-added capacity. As one of the world's largest forest companies with 570,000 hectares (1.43 million acres) of forest in Finland plus another 330,000 hectares (825,000 acres) in Uruguay and North America, UPM has the resources to create a global network of biorefineries.

UPM's breakthrough Lappeenranta Biorefinery (opened in 2015) is located next to its large Kaukas pulp and paper mill, where it has access to diverse waste streams. Its primary feedstock is crude tall oil, a by-product of pulp manufacturing from softwood. By making use of this by-product, UPM manages the wood it harvests for pulp-making more efficiently. Lappeenranta's main product is biodiesel, a sustainable alternative to fossil fuels that emits 80% less carbon dioxide than fossil fuels. It also produces renewable naphtha, a raw material for the manufacture of biochemicals and bioplastics.

Based on the initial success of this biorefinery, UPM intends to build a second refinery in Kotka, Finland, that will produce approximately 500,000 metric tons per year of advanced biofuels for use in road transportation, marine and aviation markets. According to UPM's environmental impact assessment (EIA), the new biorefinery will increase utilization of forest biowaste and residues and its fuels will decrease greenhouse gas emissions equivalent to three times those of a city the size of Helsinki. UPM is also evaluating the potential for building a third biorefinery in Germany to process hardwood residues from sustainably managed forests in Central Europe into biochemical building blocks for manufacturing textiles, renewable plastic bottles, pharmaceuticals, cosmetics, detergents and adhesives. With an annual capacity of 150,000 metric tons, it would enable significant reductions in carbon dioxide compared to fossil-fuel-based products.

UPM's advances in the field of chemistry are centered on three generic offers. The most basic of these are chemical building blocks (CBB) made from renewable lignocellulosic biomass. Used in diverse industrial goods and consumer products, these provide low carbon alternatives to petroleum-based CBBs, enabling corporate users/partners to reach their sustainability goals at cost-competitive prices. According to the Green Chemicals Blog, the market for bio-CBBs is growing at a compound annual growth rate (CAGR) of 8% and is expected to attain volumes of 3.5 million tons by 2021.

Lignin, a second bio-ingredient, is Nature's glue, with applications in a rapidly growing number of industrial products, such as epoxy resins, plastics and polyurethanes. Found in the cell walls of plants and trees, it is one of the most abundant biopolymers on Earth and an effective alternative to fossil-based raw materials like phenol. Since the global market for phenol is expected to be 11.6 million tons by 2020, demand for safer organic lignin has vast growth potential.

UPM's third line of biochemical offers include micro- and nano-fibrillar cellulose products, which are becoming effective media for biomedical research and cell-based therapies. One of its most promising products is a nanocellulose hydrogel called GrowDex™, which enhances the stability of mesenchymal stem cells used in medical research. Since it is plant-based and sterile, it is a safe medium for growing human tissue without risk of contamination. To demonstrate its versatility, the Division of Pharmaceutical Biosciences at the University of Helsinki has used GrowDex to grow a miniature liver for testing drugs. That, of course, suggests the possibility of using it to grow human tissue and spare organs using 3D cell growth. To advance such developments, UPM sends samples of GrowDex to researchers around the world.

UPM's bioeconomy partnering arrangements with peer industrial companies, startups, research institutes and universities is a wonderful example of symbiotic innovation. By helping others develop new uses for GrowDex, it has optimized utilization of its forest resources while increasing demand for its products. Further, by deriving all its products from certified forests and creating them in ways that reduce humanity's ecological footprint, it has taken symbiosis to a higher level. As President and CEO Jussi Pesonen notes, this has increased employee engagement at UPM because it inspires them with a sense of purpose to lead the world in a harmonic new direction.

Since the introduction of UPM's current business model in 2013, we have achieved a clear improvement in business performance, attractive returns for our growth investments and a truly industry-leading balance sheet. At the same time, we have seen a consistent improvement in employee engagement.

Jussi Pesonen, President and CEO[5]

Reinventing farming

In 2014, a year after the initiation of NordBio, the Norwegian fish farming company SalMar created a vision of sustainable ocean farming. Due to the declining productivity of land-based agriculture (caused by soil erosion, fresh water depletion, rising energy costs, pest resistance to chemicals and climate change) and the global depletion of wild-catch fisheries, the world faces a problem of producing enough animal protein to feed its growing population. With the world's population expected to reach 9 billion people by 2050 – a 34% increase from 2018 – the UN's Food and Agricultural Organization (FAO) projects global food supplies must increase by 70 percent.

Understanding the magnitude of this challenge, many countries have turned to fish farming in nearby coastal waters. However, raising fish in crowded coastal pens creates new problems because these are easily polluted by fish excrement and subject to predation by sea lice, which can kill fish or make them inedible to humans. To manage such predation, coastal fish farms must use chemicals that harm both the fish and their environment. As sea lice develop resistance to these chemicals, coastal fish farms must use stronger, more hazardous chemicals – an approach that ultimately poisons the commons.

Recognizing the magnitude of these challenges, SalMar's strategy is to take salmon fish farming far offshore into deeper, colder, better-oxygenated water, which fish prefer and sea lice avoid. The company's solution, called Ocean Farm, uses technology to complement Nature by creating healthy fish environments. Its first operational farm, called Ocean Farm 1, is a semi-submersible rig with a 110-meter (360-foot) wide frame equipped with high definition cameras at various depths, oxygen sensors and movable submerged feeding tubes. Launched in 2018, it is equipped with cybernetic and big data intelligence systems and sensors, including echo sounders mounted on the bottom of the rig to continually monitor the health and behavior of the fish. To maintain the health of maturing fish, a movable bulkhead continuously scrubs the farm's netting, which is designed to eliminate biofouling that can harm gill health. Sixteen movable, submerged valves disperse food at set times that allow fish to live at depths of up to 180 ft, rather than clustering them near the surface, as in other farms. With an expected 25-year lifespan, the farm is designed to resist powerful typhoons and requires only three to seven employees to operate.

Ocean Farm 1 is the first of six that SalMar has ordered at a total cost of $300 million. Designed as a full-scale pilot facility, it will also explore new technology concepts in the course of normal operations. By owning farms in groups of six or more, SalMar intends to hold one or two fallow in each production cycle to ensure the health of future crops. Each farm is designed to bring 1.5 million fish to maturity within 14 months. With such advantages, SalMar believes fish farming is feasible anywhere in the open sea.

According to a new study from the University of California, Santa Barbara, the world's current output of wild-caught seafood could be farmed in just 0.015% of the ocean's surface area. Using densely populated Indonesia as an example, it projects just 1% of that country's suitable ocean area could produce more than 24 million metric tons of fish per year – enough to increase its per capita seafood consumption six-fold.[6] Based on this study, clusters of SalMar deep water fish farms operating around the world could feasibly produce enough affordable protein to sustainably meet global demand by 2050.

By working in partnership with Nature rather than trying to control it with chemicals, SalMar embraces the best features of Nordic ethical and ecological values. By thinking foremost about the health of its fish and the ocean environment in which they are raised, it is taking farming to a dynamic new level.

> High ethical and moral standards form the basis for developing an even stronger focus on safeguarding the environment that ... we are the temporary custodians of. We shall not deplete the environment, but ensure that we pass it on unimpaired to the next generation. This is our shared social responsibility, and everything we do must stand up to public scrutiny both today and in the future.
>
> SalMar, "Sustainability in Everything we do."[7]

SalMar's shares, traded on the Oslo Borse, gave it a market value of roughly NOK49 billion ($5.1 billion) at yearend 2019. Its principal owner, Kvera A/S, is a private holding company. This protects SalMar from predatory takeover bids by other food companies, thus enabling it to maintain its ethical culture and long-term symbiotic vision. In further support of that vision, SalMar's 2019 financial statement reflects a healthy balance sheet with a debt/equity ratio of 38.6% and a return on equity (ROE) of 27.0% – strong results for a company in the midst of an aggressive capital spending program.

Reinventing food processing

Chr. Hansen, founded in Denmark during the 19th century as a food processing company, is today a global nutrition-based biosciences company, whose product innovations are derived from more than 30,000 microbial strains. These "good bacteria" enable farmers and food manufacturers to produce more with less while also reducing the use of chemicals and other synthetic additives. Based on its progressive culture and progress in developing healthy plant, animal and human food systems, it was rated number one in the 2019 Global 100: a list of the world's most sustainable companies presented each year at the annual meeting of the World Economic Forum.

In 2013, the year NordBio was launched, Chr. Hansen introduced its "Nature's no. 1" strategy, which aims to increase food production while reducing the environmental impacts of production by improving plant and animal health. To enhance plant health, for example, it has developed bacteria that improve soil quality, protect crops and improve yields without chemicals. Because many of its microbes create symbiotic relationships with target crops, where both plant and soil benefit, they promote healthy, long-term feedback cycles rather than fleeting short-term gains. According to the American Academy of Microbiology, such solutions could improve plant health, increase crop productivity by 20% and reduce fertilizer and pesticide requirements by 20% within 20 years.[8]

In the field of animal health, Chr. Hansen offers probiotics that improve digestion, resist disease and promote the wellbeing of livestock. As natural alternatives to antibiotics, they improve animal health at lower costs. In addition, they reduce the risk of creating bacterial antibiotic resistance, which can be dangerous to both animals and humans. Considered together, the beneficial effects of both plant and animal product lines flow from farms to consumers and public health – all of which have positive economic effects.

To advance its global leadership in plant and animal health, Hansen launched in 2017 a second generation of bioprotective cultures tailored to warm-climate countries with less developed cooling infrastructure. By

looking beyond its largest markets in the world's leading industrial economies to the health of developing areas of Africa, Asia and Latin America,
these new cultures aim to improve the planet's biome and ability to feed a
growing population. In addition, they will reduce the need for expensive
fossil fuels, chemical fertilizers and insecticides, which are leading sources
of ecological devastation.

In Chr. Hansen's original field of food processing, it provides natural
microbial and enzymatic ingredients to improve the taste, nutritional
value, health benefits and shelf life of dairy products, meats and wine.
Working with diverse global partners in food growing and processing, it
has the most complete offering of probiotic solutions of any company in
this critical industry. With R&D spending at 7.4% of sales during the fiscal
year 2019, Chr. Hansen is committed to remaining a leader in this symbiotic field of producing safe, healthy food in ways that improve the health
of soil, plants and animal life.

As evidence of this commitment, more than 80% of Chr. Hansen's revenue is derived from products that contribute to the UN's Global Goals of
reducing hunger, promoting health and sustainable production. Because
these goals are integrated into corporate strategy, its contributions in these
areas are measured annually and verified independently as part of its regu-
lar reporting. This expression of caring for people and the planet is a matter
of pride to employees, who respond by being deeply engaged in its progressive, life-affirming culture of innovation.

The effects of employee engagement and strong customer partnerships
are reflected in the value of Chr. Hansen's stock, which increased more
than fivefold between its June 2010 public offering and yearend 2019. With
a 32% ROE and a strong operating cash flow, Chr. Hansen is another outstanding example of NordBio's symbiotic vision of using Nordic biological expertise to strengthen both the region's economy and the long-term
health of the world economy.

Our strategy is called Nature's no. 1, and it has been the foundation
of the results achieved over the past five years. The new sub-heading,
Sustainably, refers to the sustainability of the strategy and business
model, as well as our positive impact on sustainability and the UN
Sustainability Development Goals.

Chr. Hansen Annual Report, 2017/18[9]

Reinventing power generation

Since the start of the industrial revolution more than 250 years ago, fossil fuels have been the primary energy source for the developed world. Over the past five decades, however, as the prices of these fuels became more volatile and their adverse ecological effects more apparent, other sources of power generation (primarily nuclear) began to develop. Seeing an opportunity in this field, Vestas entered the wind turbine industry in 1979.

At the time, wind energy seemed a symbiotic solution because wind was globally abundant and could be harnessed with minimal ecological impacts. Vestas' challenge was to do this in a cost-effective way that could become scalable for major markets. Four decades later, Vestas' founding ideal has become a reality. As the world's largest manufacturer of wind turbines, its most efficient ones now generate electricity at less than half the cost of natural gas. Its turbines are also more cost-effective than nuclear energy, which has been losing global market share due to the high expenses of plant construction and the hazards of storing radioactive spent fuel.

Given the ecological and cost advantages of its turbines, demand for Vestas' technology is surging. To keep up, it now manufactures in every major market including the European Union, China, India, the US and Latin America. At mid-year 2019, with more than 66,000 turbines operating worldwide on five continents, Vestas' order book remains full. With nearly 25,000 employees operating in more than 80 countries, its 2019 global market share was 22% – up from 16% in 2017. On the strength of its technology leadership, that share looks likely to grow, constrained only by Vestas' ability to keep up with demand.

Today the fastest-growing segment of the wind power market is offshore windfarms, where developers can construct taller turbines with bigger blades that can access higher wind velocities. Thanks to Vestas' Danish partner Ørsted, which is the world's largest developer of offshore windfarms, it operates on the cutting edge of this business. In September 2018, the two companies inaugurated the world's most powerful offshore windfarm in the North Sea: the 659-megawatt (MW) Walney Extension, a facility that surpassed their previous record project, the 630-MW London Array.

To coordinate Vestas' growing global network of wind power stations, the company introduced in 2011 its "Firestorm" supercomputer (then one of the world's fastest), allowing it to offer the most complete end-to-end service of any global energy company. With embedded artificial intel-ligence, Firestorm determines the best position for each new windmill, monitors weather forecasts, predicts the output of windfarm operations on an hourly to day-ahead basis and provides feedback that enables service teams to quickly provide maintenance as needed.

With such data, Firestorm collects valuable information for the develop-ment of future generations of wind turbines. Vestas' new EnVentus turbines are a good example. Using a modular design approach, their large rotors can reach stronger wind speeds enabling their annual energy production to increase 30% compared to earlier models. With such efficiency, the advan-tages of wind power relative to fossil fuels and nuclear energy are becom-ing ever more favorable.

Following its introduction of Firestorm in June 2011, Vestas shares appreciated more than five-fold in the seven-and-a-half years through yearend 2019. On the strength of growing customer demand and operat-ing margins, it ended that year with more cash than debt on its balance sheet. With a return on equity (ROE) of nearly 22%, it has the financial strength to maintain and increase its technology lead – a symbiotic benefit to Denmark, its global customers and shareholders.

> We have stayed in the lead, reporting solid results, and delivered on our strategic objectives to grow faster than the market, deliver best-in-class margins, and offer the lowest cost of energy solutions to our customers.
> Anders Runevad, Group President and CEO, 2017[10]

Looking to the future, large corporate energy buyers have joined munici-palities in demanding increased access to wind power as investments in local resiliency. In the US, a consortium of more than 200 large US com-panies called the Renewable Energy Buyers Alliance (REBA) has been using its collective purchasing power to bring more renewable power on line. With an ambitious goal to catalyze an additional 60 GW of new renewable energy by 2025, and a corps of leadership companies, including Google, Johnson & Johnson, Disney, Walmart and General Motors, it has the power to advance its agenda in spite of resistance from domestic fossil fuel and utility companies.

Given these symbiotic advantages, Vestas robustly supports NordBio's agenda of making more effective uses of Earth's natural resources (of which wind is one). Even though it does not use bio-innovation to generate value, it may do more in the long run to reduce the industrial world's dependence on hazardous fossil fuels than any technology so far developed.

Public–private partnerships

What started in Kalundborg more than 50 years ago has become a standard in the Nordic world with governments and private companies working together to provide essential public services, such as health care and education, plus long-term development projects like NordBio. In all such cases, the ideal is to have each partner do what it does best – with governments attending to common interests and companies using their skills to find sustainable, cost-effective solutions.

In the case of NordBio, the Nordic Council of Ministers had a grand vision of using the region's emerging skills in bio-innovation as a means of optimizing its most abundant natural resources to develop a stable economy for the benefit of all citizens. In doing so, it provided a coordinated framework for collaboration that reached across national and functional boundaries to engage all generations, including schoolchildren, in this quest.

As a strategy, this approach offers a wonderful example of the operating leverage that occurs when people become inspired by a meaningful vision of the future (as described in Appendix One). With NordBio, that vision concerns the wellbeing of society, the ecosphere and future generations – goals that engage people's highest (spiritual) thinking capacities and encourages them to explore new technologies and circular economy solutions.

The effectiveness of this approach is evident in a cascade of beneficial outcomes and feedbacks: from Nordic leadership in the fields of bio-innovation, industrial ecology and renewable energy to their beneficial effects on Nordic productivity and export revenues, through to the health of regional economies and their capacities to support government investments in the health, education and well-being of Nordic citizens. This cascade, in turn, generates a reinforcing cycle as healthy, educated Nordic citizens willingly join to improve the region's quality of life.

Considered as a whole, this reinforcing cycle of leverage points has generated a region with the world's highest general standard of living – an outcome Nordic countries have achieved with remarkably little debt.

To further the goals of public participation and symbiotic visioning, employees serve on the boards of companies in Denmark, Norway and Sweden. In addition, when companies and governments in these countries report their financial results to the public, they are required to include non-financial data on their ecological and social impacts. The same spirit of information sharing and collaboration applies to wage negotiations where employers, union representatives and governments bargain at the national level based on common interests and a shared belief that when all groups perform their functions well, society will function harmoniously.

Because of such symbiotic co-operation, Nordic workers are among the best paid and most secure in the world. According to the International Trade Union Confederation's 2019 Global Rights Index, all five Nordic countries were rated in the highest (Group 1) bracket out of 142 nations surveyed. By comparison, the US was given a low (Group 4) rating due to its "systematic violation of rights."[11]

This same spirit of co-operation and partnership also extends to the delivery of important public services, such as education, health care and maintenance of essential infrastructure. Municipal governments in Sweden, for example, contract with private companies to operate publicly funded charter schools (friskola) under long-term arrangements that ensure proper care of the facility and service to the community. In such cases, the municipality moves from being a *provider* of public service to a *regulator* with the authority to define the curriculum while letting companies compete for the management work.

Although this system of public–private partnership has worked well in the fields of health care and infrastructure, it has had mixed results in Sweden where children from high socioeconomic backgrounds have had better access to charter schools than those in immigrant enclaves. Because of this access issue, average test scores for Swedish 15-year-olds suffered the worst decline of any developed country for the decade through 2013 under the Program for International Student Assessment (PISA). Although the 2018 test results were back above developed country (OECD) averages, they excluded students who were not proficient in Swedish – an issue Sweden's government is trying to correct by providing better housing and more services to its immigrant population, including mentorship programs for children at risk. By acknowledging its failure and pragmatically reassessing its approach to the education of immigrant children, the Swedish government has demonstrated its impressive capacity for multiple-loop learning (Chapter Three).

Aside from this anomaly, most Nordic public–private collaborations have added to the success and sustainability of the region's economies because they operate from shared symbiotic visioning and values. Whether originating from the Nordic Council of Ministers or individual government agencies, they succeed by empowering local citizens, organizations and companies to create meaningful advances in sustainable enterprise.

One such venture allowed Denmark's Samsø Island to become a global exemplar of community-based sustainable energy production. The story of its transition began in 1997 when Denmark's Ministry for Environment invited local municipalities to submit ideas for generating 100% of their energy from renewables. After winning the competition, Samsø got public funding to develop a master plan. Fulfillment of the plan was left to residents of the island and to private investors. Ten years later, Samsø had eleven privately owned onshore wind turbines and ten offshore ones, five of which were privately owned and five owned by the municipality. Today, in combination with solar and biomass, the island generates more energy than it needs, with the surplus exported to the mainland for extra revenue.

On a larger national scale, Finland uses two public organizations to advance its quest to become the world's first circular economy: Sitra, a National Fund for Research and Development operating under the supervision of Finland's parliament; and Business Finland, directed by the Finnish Ministry for Employment and the Economy.

Sitra's primary goals are to advance a "carbon-neutral circular economy" and develop Finland's capacity "to renew itself," which it does through direct investments in private enterprise and participating in forums, such as the annual Slush events in Helsinki. With a public endowment valued at €933 million ($1.1 billion) at yearend 2018, it has the financial strength to leverage numerous promising private sector experiments. Business Finland (formerly known as Tekes) finances early stage projects with the goal of transforming them into viable businesses. With offices in Silicon Valley, New York City and other innovation hubs, it operates much like a venture capital firm to "promote the competitiveness of Finnish industry ... by assisting in the creation of world-class technology and technological know-how." Given their common goals, these two public organizations offer companies valuable funding and advice at different stages of development.

The galvanizing spirit of Nordic responsibility

The important message of this chapter concerns the depth of symbiotic thinking in the development of Nordic economies and the willingness of Nordic people to take personal responsibility for making the world a better place. As described in Chapter Three, this spirit is imbued from childhood onwards through a philosophy of life-long learning (*Bildung*) that widens an individual's circle of belonging – from family to Nature to a love of democracy and eventually to the well-being of future generations.

We find evidence of this spirit everywhere: in Nordic accounting systems, in the student-led, change-the-world Slush movement, in regional commitments to the UN's 2030 Sustainable Development Goals and in Nordic circular economy leadership. While we can marvel at Nordic technical achievements in renewable energy and circular economy innovations, this is the source of their achievements and the reason they keep advancing in the field of sustainable development.

As economic ideals, these visions and values reverse those of mainstream neoclassical economic thinking. Rather than putting gross domestic product (GDP) and profit ahead of people and the planet, Nordic people take the opposite approach. By looking first to the health of society and Nature, which are the primary sources GDP and profit, they get better outcomes in all dimensions: healthier people, more robust ecosystems and a more prosperous economy.

In a 2017 progress report progress on the Bioeconomy Initiative, the Nordic Council of Ministers observed that by the year 2050, the world will need a 50% increase in energy and food production compared to 2017. To accomplish this, they concluded: "(We) may not need to increase our usage of (natural resources) by 50%. We do, however, need to be 50% smarter and more sustainable."[12]

Notes

1 Donella Meadows. 1994. "Envisioning a sustainable world," *Third Biennial Meeting of the International Society for Ecological Economics*. October 24–8,

San Jose, Costa Rica. The Academy for Systems Change. Available from: http://donellameadows.org/archives/envisioning-a-sustainable-world/ [Accessed June 29, 2020].

2 The Nordic Bioeconomy Initiative. 2019. Available from: https://nordicagrire search.org/wp-content/uploads/2014/04/NBI-strategydoc-ENG.pdf. p. 2.

3 Lene Lange et al. 2015. "Development of the Nordic bioeconomy," Danish Technical University. p. 16. Available from: http://orbit.dtu.dk/files/1406 39248/Development_of_the_Nordic_Bioeconomy_Lange_et_al_2016.pdf [Accessed June 29, 2020].

4 Nordic Council of Ministers. 2017. Gíslason, Stefán (Editor) and Bragadóttir, Hrafnhildur (Editor). Available from: https://issuu.com/nordic_council_of _ministers/docs/tn2017526web [Accessed June 29, 2020].

5 UPM Group. *UPM Annual Report 2017*, p. 9. Available from: http://hugin.info/ 165629/R/2172145/837189.pdf [Accessed June 29, 2020].

6 Rebecca R Gentry et al. 2017. "Mapping the global potential for marine aquaculture," *Nature Ecology & Evolution 1.* 1: pp. 1317–24. Available from: https://www.nature.com/articles/s41559-017-0257-9 [Accessed June 29, 2020].

7 The SalMar Culture, Shared Values, Shared Culture. https://www.salmar.no/ en/the-salmar-culture-shared-values-shared-culture/

8 Ann Reid and Shannon E Greene. 2012. "How microbes can help feed the world," *American Academy of Microbiology.* December. Available from: https:// www.ncbi.nlm.nih.gov/books/NBK559436/.

9 Chr. Hansen Annual Report 2017/18. p. 7.

10 Vestas Annual Report 2017. Remarks by Anders Runevad, Group President and CEO. p. 5. Available from: https://www.vestas.com/~/media/vestas/in vestor/investor%20pdf/financial%20reports/2017/q4/2017_annual_report .pdf

11 International Trade Union Confederation (ITUC) Global Rights Index 2019. https://www.ituc-csi.org/IMG/pdf/2019-06-ituc-global-rights-index-2019- report-en-2.pdf

12 S Gislason and H Bragadottir. 2017. *The Nordic Bioeconomy Initiative: Final Report*, p. 8. Available from: https://norden.divaportal.org/smash/get/diva2: 1065456/FULLTEXT01.pdf [Accessed June 29, 2020].

7

TOWARD A MORE CONSCIOUS ECONOMY

The Nordic countries have made the most out of the industrial era. We had a vision and built some of the most open, free, egalitarian, safe, stable, and progressive societies the world has ever seen. We are also among the happiest people in the world... But where do we go next?

Lene Rachael Andersen, Futurist, 2018[1]

Nordic countries have always been at the forefront in working with environmental indicators, accountings and modeling. It was therefore a natural step for us to examine what the economics of ecosystems and biodiversity encompass in the Nordic context.

Nordic Council of Ministers, 2012[2]

Consciousness is an emergent property of human life. At a basic level, it encompasses anything we are aware of at a given moment based on our experience and learning. At a higher level, it includes our willingness to absorb new information (feedback) and our capacity to use that to modify our worldview (rewire our brains). At the highest level, it draws on our moral capacity to empathize, to sense that we are part of a larger universal whole that we may not fully understand, but which has an emotional or spiritual value to us (such as the health of ecosystems, the biosphere and future generations).

In Nordic countries, public consciousness is grounded in their philosophy of education (Bildung), which aims to endow every citizen with an awareness of their belonging to a larger interdependent whole. While not everybody takes such learning to advanced levels of consciousness, most have an awareness that living in harmony with the biosphere and each other is preferable to economic practices that subordinate people and Nature to the goals of growing gross domestic product (GDP).

Such elements of consciousness informed the evolution of Kalundborg's Symbiosis, as described in Chapter One. No government body told the citizens of that small city to collaborate as they did in creating the world's first circular economy. Instead, they acted out of a shared concern for the future of their municipality, their country, their impacts on Nature and the wellbeing of future generations in a resource-constrained world.[3] As their spontaneous collaborative processes evolved and prospered, other Nordic communities began to embrace Kalundborg's model.

Over time, this progression put Nordic economies on a different trajectory than their GDP-driven industrial peers. This is especially visible since the 1992 Rio de Janeiro Earth Summit when climate change emerged as a prominent global issue. From that time forward, Nordic countries committed to reducing their carbon emissions by resolutely pursuing green growth agendas. Combined with their fiscal reforms during that era, this pursuit gave shape to the Nordic Model as we know it today.

Looking back on this time, it is evident that such broad spectrum consciousness played a critical role in the Nordic region's success. This is a difficult concept for people and cultures accustomed to linear cause and effect (bottom line) thinking, but it is a proven pathway to humanity's highest spiritual intelligence (SQ) – the intelligence that gives purpose and meaning to our lives.

Nordic capacity for sensing limits and opportunities

By engaging these higher thinking capacities, Nordic cultures have developed an instinctive *sense of limits* concerning Nature's biological carrying capacity and human endurance – instincts that are manifest in their pro-gressive ecological practices and universal safety nets. Integral to these intuitions is an adaptive capacity to *sense opportunity* – a quality that explains their global leadership in renewable energy, biotechnology and circular economy solutions.

Considered together, these sensing abilities lead to better strategic think-ing. We find tangible evidence of this at multiple levels: from the large number of Nordic companies named each year to the Global 100 of sus-tainability leaders (Appendix Two) to the spontaneous innovations of the entrepreneurial Nordic startup community and the progressive policies of the Nordic Council of Ministers.

The cohesiveness of Nordic eco-centric thinking, as mentioned earlier, has deep cultural roots. Long before the 19th-century emergence of *Bildung* as a holistic learning philosophy, Nordic people felt a strong affiliation with Nature – one reaching back more than a thousand years to Viking sagas, which regarded everything in Nature as physically and spiritually con-nected. Later, during the 16th-century Reformation, Nordic people became exposed to the similarly inclusive (egalitarian) values of Martin Luther. When these mores blended, they fed a culture where life-affirming values, visions and goals were widely shared, freely discussed and acted upon.

According to Robert H. Nelson, author of *Lutheranism and the Nordic Spirit of Social Democracy*, Luther's values advanced this capacity for dialogue by endorsing complete equality between men and women.[4] By ensuring that everyone has a voice in matters of common interest and governance, such openness facilitates an awareness of whole systems – from ecological limits to opportunities for remediation and advancement (renewable energy, cir-cular economy solutions).

As if to put an exclamation point on the Nordic region's long-standing affiliation with Nature, the popular 19th-century Norwegian playwright and poet, Henrik Ibsen, distilled it into a single word: "friluftsliv." Translated as "open-air living," it describes the value of spending time outdoors, espe-cially in wilderness areas, for spiritual and physical wellbeing.

The idea of Nature as a "spiritual sanctuary" was later amplified by the Norwegian philosopher Arne Naess, who coined the term "deep ecology." As an idiom, it drew an essential distinction between *shallow* anthropo-centric thinking of modern society and the *deep* eco-centric insights required to live in harmony with Nature. Conceived in the early 1970s, a time when human economies were beginning to seriously overstep Nature's biological limits, Naess' writing drew attention to the interdependence of all life on Earth. Tellingly, from this point forward, Nordic countries became more conscious of their ecological footprints and began to plan with Nature in mind, as seen in Kalundborg and more broadly illustrated in Appendix Three.

At its core, Naess's goal was to awaken humanity to the reality that we are merely one of many interdependent species within the planetary web of life rather than being separate from and above Nature. As such, it advanced a basic premise of the life-mimicking model: that human cultures and political economies are sub-systems of life rather than super-systems that transcend life.

Considered together, the foregoing social and ecological roots of Nordic philosophy have become core values in modern systems thinking. While Bildung unites these values in creative ways, they are fundamentally (if latently) present in all cultures through humanity's innate biophilic instincts. The challenge before us today is to present them anew and embed them in renewed systems of political-economic governance.

One of the ways Nordic countries do this is to infuse their holistic, life-mimicking values into their accounting practices. As mentioned in Chapter Six, Nordic companies and governments routinely put ecological and social data in reports alongside financial results – a practice that naturally embeds holistic thinking into business and official management practices.

Holistic policy-making

To understand the importance and ethical significance of such accounting practices, and the related 2013 Nordic Bioeconomy Initiative, it is important to know how regional government policy-making works and the moral authority it carries among member countries.

Essential dialogue typically begins locally, then works its way up to the Nordic Council – a "forum for debate, information exchange and opinion forming" focused on matters of common interest, such as culture, education, citizens' rights, environment, natural resources, business and welfare." Because council members are elected from regional parliaments, their opinions carry weight in regional legislatures and in inter-parliamentary co-operation; however, they do not have formal power in policy-making for the region as a whole.

That ultimate power rests with the Nordic Council of Ministers. As the official body for inter-governmental co-operation in the region, it seeks unified solutions premised on an understanding that the five countries can achieve more together than by working on their own. Because decisions taken by ministerial councils must be unanimous, when the councils are aligned, as they were for the Bioeconomy Initiative and the Strategic Plan on accounting practices, they have considerable weight as directives for political-economic policy and action.

One of the most progressive actions of the Nordic Council of Ministers was its 2019 initiative called "Nordic Solutions to Global Challenges." In keeping with *Bildung*'s ideal of widening one's circles of belonging, it looks beyond the Nordic region to the long-term health of the global political economy. Created as a three-year initiative to share Nordic knowledge and experience in vital areas related to the UN's Sustainable Development Goals, the initiative has "six flagship projects spanning sustainable town planning, regional energy co-operation, investments in gender equality, sustainable food production, smart welfare and climate solutions."

> These Nordic solutions will be effective tools in our common work to reach the United Nations Sustainability Goals by 2030.
>
> Nordic Council of Ministers, 2019[5]

As further evidence of the Nordic region's global consciousness, Finland and Denmark have developed national circular economy strategies, whose objectives and planning processes they now actively share with the world. Finland, for example, sponsored the first (2017) and third (2019) World Circular Economy Forums in Helsinki and its national innovation fund (Sitra) helped to organize the 2018 Forum in Tokyo. Denmark's *Strategy for Circular Economy*, published in 2018, is a public document that can be viewed anywhere.

Reflecting this shared sense of systemic awareness and concern for the good of the whole, Nordic countries are leaders in the 2018 Good Country Index – a balance sheet of data gathered from the UN and other international organizations that measures what each country on Earth contributes to the common good of humanity, and what it takes away, relative to its size. Out of 153 countries surveyed, the four largest Nordic countries were solidly in the top ten with Finland rated first, Sweden fourth, Denmark sixth and Norway eighth. Although a champion of democracy and sustainability, Iceland was rated 36th because it has not contributed as much "to the greater good of humanity" as its Nordic neighbors. Nevertheless, it was ranked above the US (40th), which was marked down due to its low scores on matters of "International Peace and Security" plus "Planet and Climate."[6]

Companies making it happen

The faith Nordic governments have in creating ambitious goals and policies is justified by the innovative ways Nordic companies take up the challenge. As mentioned earlier, this is evident in the large number of Nordic companies named to the annual Global 100 list of sustainability leaders since 2010 and the number of Nordic startups working in the fields of cleantech and circular economy solutions. By working together, all parties derive multiple wins: first, by profitably solving real world problems; second, by advancing the "Nordic brand" for product integrity and finally by generating taxable incomes that support regional safety nets. Since these safety nets create a rich supply of advanced human skills for Nordic companies, the process has become a powerful reinforcing loop.

Neste, a mid-sized company that is 50.1% owned by Finland's government, is an excellent example of this multiple win dynamic. Moved by declining margins for oil refining and concerns about global climate change, it began in 2007 to transform itself from a conventional refiner to become the world's largest producer of renewable biodiesel refined from recycled organic waste and residues. Thanks to its innovation, leadership and growth, it ended 2019 with a return on equity of roughly 34% and a strong balance sheet with more cash than debt. From 2009, when its first biorefinery opened in Porvoo, Finland, to yearend 2019, its shares grew in value more than eightfold. With three operating refineries (Finland, Holland, Singapore), it produced 2.7 million metric tons of renewable diesel and aviation fuel in 2018. With expansions underway in Singapore, it expects to generate 4.5 million metric tons by 2022. As an increasingly effective global leader in biofuel production, it has been listed in the Global 100 list of corporate sustainability leaders every year since 2008, coming in second in 2018 and third in 2019 – an extraordinary achievement.

With a corporate vision of "creating a healthier planet for our children," Neste looks to the outer edges of humanity's circles of belonging. Its corporate culture is guided by a strong vision and a widely shared belief among employees that there is an urgent global need for profit-making renewable energy solutions that can grow anywhere without public subsidy. To optimize employee engagement and entrepreneurship in this quest, Neste gives its personnel authority to self-organize and network in pursuit of greater efficiencies.

Writing in Neste's 2017 annual report, CEO Matti Leovonen touches on this very point:

> We succeed by dividing our challenges into smaller parts and assigning people responsibility to complete their work … Our employees know that they are making a difference … so it is easy for them to find meaning in their work … We are networking with other operators more actively than before, for agile co-operation is the only way to succeed in a world that is changing more and more rapidly.[7]

Demand for Neste's biodiesel has grown rapidly for two compelling reasons. First, as a cleaner fuel, it improves engine performance while reducing service and maintenance costs. Second, its renewable fuels lower greenhouse gas emissions by 50% to 90% over their lifecycles (from production through distribution to final use). According to company reports, these reductions amounted to 7.9 million metric tons in 2018. With significant new investment in renewables production coming on line, Neste expects to double its customers' greenhouse gas (GHG) reductions by 2022.

We announced in December 2018 that we are investing EUR 1.4 billion to increase our renewable products production capacity in Singapore. This brings our total renewable product capacity close to 4.5 Mt annually in 2022 from the 2.9 Mt today, and enables us to double our GHG reduction impact from the 2018 level.

Neste Sustainability Report, 2018[8]

Looking to the future, Neste's strategy is to grow its renewable product line in three waves: first, to continue its leadership in renewable diesel, which is expected to quadruple to approximately 20 million tons by 2030;

second, to develop the renewable jet fuel market and become a leader in aviation decarbonization and third, to become a leader in renewable polymers and chemicals for consumer brands. To reach these goals, company R&D is presently focused on algae and forest waste, which will significantly expand its access to raw materials.

With a market capitalization at yearend 2019 of €23.4 billion ($25.9 billion), Neste has become a substantial asset of Finland's government. Based on the government's 50.1% ownership interest, its share was worth €11.7 billion at yearend 2019, equivalent to 21% of Finland's 2019 budget of €55.5 billion. Considering Neste's planned production growth, the rising global demand for its fuels and its high return on equity, the government's shareholdings are likely to continue growing faster than its budget, creating a substantial fiscal buffer for future generations.

While the government of Finland's half ownership of Neste's shares may seem overbearing to investors outside the Nordic world, corporate management has total operating control. For company management, the advantage of having the government as a supportive, but otherwise passive partner, is the protection it affords from hostile takeovers by larger global fossil fuel companies. For the government of Finland, its share of Neste's rapidly growing stream of dividends was worth €255 million in 2019 ($281 million), a significant source of revenue that strengthens its capacity to maintain strong universal safety nets. The strength of those safety nets, in turn, is a benefit to Neste as it provides the company with a cohort of educated, skilled employees whose health care expenses are covered.

Novo Nordisk, another Nordic sustainability champion, is one of the world's most profitable pharmaceutical companies with an astonishing record of innovation. Beyond its earlier noted exceptional growth, its most notable legacy is the Novo Nordisk Foundation. Founded in 1922 along with the company itself, the foundation has catalyzed a revolution in Nordic bioinnovation through its grant-making and venture capital investing. With an endowment valued in excess of $50 billion at yearend 2019, it is by far the largest foundation in Denmark and one of the biggest in the world.

The principal assets of the foundation are Novo Nordisk itself, Novozymes (a sister company, spun off in 2000) and Novo Holdings A/S (a subsidiary company with investments in more than 75 other companies). Thanks to the strong investment returns on these assets, the foundation generated

$1.7 billion during 2018, of which more than $300 million was distributed in grants and funding in the fields of biomedicine and biotechnology. With such spending power and influence, the foundation has been a major catalyst to the Nordic region's global leadership in bio-innovation and circular economy strategies.

Aside from Novo Nordisk and Novozymes, holding company assets are spread among promising companies through Novo Ventures (a venture capital fund) and Novo Seeds (a biotech startup fund). Foundation grants support a network of research centers including a center for basic metabolic research, a center for stem cell biology, a center for protein research and a center for biosustainability in collaboration with Danish Technical University (DTU). Considered together, these research centers have a powerful influence on advancing biotechnology in the Nordic region. Their very success as centers of bio-innovation and circular economy leadership inspired the Nordic Council of Ministers to introduce in 2014 the Nordic Bioeconomy Initiative.

The foundation's endowment growth is derived from its two major assets. Since the year 2000, when Novo Nordisk spun off Novozymes, the shares of the two companies have produced exceptional growth. For the 20-year period through yearend 2019, the shares of Novo Nordisk appreciated more than 21-fold and those of Novozymes by nearly 10-fold. In addition to these core assets, Novo Holding A/S has generated significant returns on its Novo Ventures and Novo Seeds investments. According to its 2018 annual report, these generated average annual returns of 18% for the ten years ending in that year.[9]

The secret to the foundation's success, as with its two primary holdings, is a philosophy of management centered on life. By focusing on improving conditions for human and biospheric life, the foundation generates reinforcing cycles of positive economic and ecological feedback. As a leading example of management by means (MBM), this strategy boosts the productive capacities of people and Nature, which are the primary sources of economic value creation.

There is a recurring pattern here that we find throughout this book. Whether talking about companies or economies, life-mimicking cultures that consciously care for the good of the whole are more productive than those motivated by linear pursuits of profit and GDP.

Leverage points

By imagining companies and economies as sub-systems of life, Nordic cultures start with an immediate advantage. By seeing the world as it is, rather than a contrived platform for generating GDP, they gain a more coherent sense of its ecological limits in addition to more creative pathways into the future. As illustrated in Appendix One, this fundamental insight naturally leads to life-affirming goal setting, which inspires the creation of life-mimicking cultures, which in turn generates life-centered learning and innovation and enables people and institutions to adapt as the world around them changes.

Nordic Bildung, a futurist think tank, provides a wonderful example of employing such leverage points. To address the increasing risks that world GDP growth is outrunning Earth's biological carrying capacity, it has developed a coherent strategy for restoring systemic balance. Co-founded by Lene Rachel Andersen, an economist and lead author of *The Nordic Secret* (extensively cited in Chapter Three), its approach is to continuously renew the region's life-mimicking culture, which has been the source of its global sustainability leadership. To achieve this goal, Nordic Bildung reaches across multiple domains – ranging from ethics, aesthetics and purpose to science, technology, production and the use of power – recognizing that these are key leverage points in the region's circular economy and technology development.[10]

By addressing these leverage points, Andersen aims to accelerate the development of four transformative technologies: biotech, infotech (digitalization), nanotech (material science) and cognitive sciences (artificial intelligence), which she refers to with the acronym BINC. In an article written with Steen Rasmussen, a research professor at the US Santa Fe Institute and the University of Southern Denmark (later published by the World Economic Forum), she reckons the transformative potential of these new technologies "could be as drastic as the differences between the Stone Age and the Bronze Age, or from agricultural society to the scientific age of industry."[11] Although a bold prophecy in today's uncertain and ecologically vulnerable world, the technologies she describes are advancing quickly in Nordic countries motivated by a conscious realization that the continuation of life on Earth as we know it depends on our collective abilities to live and work in closer harmony with Nature and each other.

As noted earlier, the Nordic region's global leadership in renewable energy has been accompanied by widespread use of digitalization – a time- and energy-saving technology that enables communications and electricity distribution networks to become more connected and efficient. Nordic advances in this field are reflected in the 2017 Digital Evolution Index, which emerged from a global survey by Mastercard and the Fletcher School at Tufts University. According to the index, the most advanced digital economies in the world at that time were Norway (1), Sweden (2), Switzerland (3), Denmark (4) and Finland (5).[12]

Of the four BINC disciplines, cognitive sciences (artificial intelligence) are the least developed in Nordic countries relative to innovation leaders in the US, China and Japan. Nevertheless, the region's large manufacturing companies have been rapidly catching up in order to maintain their competitive positions in world markets.

This catch-up phase is proceeding on three fronts: first via private consultancies, such as Combient, a joint venture of 28 large companies in Finland and Sweden seeking to advance their capacities in artificial intelligence (AI), blockchain and the Internet of Things (IoT); second, through nonprofits like Stockholm's Nordic AI Artificial Intelligence Institute and third, by means of government action coordinated by the Nordic Council of Ministers for Digitalization.

Such collaborative networking has been an enduring catalyst in the Nordic economy. As in Kalundborg, it feeds on a spirit of mutual trust and shared goals centered on the social, ecological and financial health of the region. In this spirit, consultants at Combient engage daily with executives and experts among associated companies to discover "common needs." Then, using their accumulated knowledge, they "test and realize new solutions to meet those needs" and finally circulate the knowledge gained for the benefit of everyone. Unlike the more proprietary approach used in other markets, this speeds the development of AI and shared learning.

As shown in Table 7.1 (below), BINC technologies are now ubiquitous among Nordic manufacturers – especially those in the Global 100 of sustainability leaders. Of these, the two most widely shared are infotech and AI since these accelerate adaptive learning. Biotech and nanotech, although more content-related, are equally important because they enable humanity to understand and partner with Nature in innovative new ways.

Table 7.1 Nordic leaders in BINC technologies

Company	Country	BINC Technologies	World Leader
Atlas Copco	Sweden	Infotech, nanotech, AI	Industrial equipment
Equinor	Norway	Biotech, infotech, nanotech, AI	Diversified energy
Fortum	Finland	Infotech, AI	Diversified clean energy
Chr. Hansen	Denmark	Biotech, infotech, nanotech, AI	Natural solutions (food)
Neste	Finland	Biotech, infotech, AI	Renewable energy
Novozymes	Denmark	Biotech, infotech, nanotech, AI	Enzymes technology
Novo Nordisk	Denmark	Biotech, infotech, AI	Pharmaceuticals
Ørsted	Denmark	Infotech, AI	Offshore windfarms
Sandvik	Sweden	Infotech, nanotech, AI	Materials technology
Tomra	Norway	Biometrics, infotech, AI	Recycling, food sorting
UPM	Finland	Biotech, infotech, nanotech, AI	Wood-derived biofuels
Vestas	Denmark	Infotech, AI	Wind turbines

Nanotech, for example, has enabled Nordic companies to expand into the field of micro-fabrication, a method of making better products with less waste of energy and materials. Sandvik, a Swedish manufacturer, uses it to develop materials for the 3D printing of machine tools and Atlas Copco uses it to produce construction tools. In the field of medical research, UPM and Novozymes have used nanotech to develop biopolymers from wood materials to produce GrowDex™, a hydrogel that has multiple applications in medical research, including customized drug treatment. For the world's huge agriculture industry, Chr. Hansen has used nanotech to develop pro-biotic solutions for crop protection and to safeguard livestock from disease and infestation.

All of the foregoing companies are global technology leaders, as well as market share leaders in their fields, based on their abilities to generate sustainable value. In addition, all have strong balance sheets and produce substantial operating cash flows. As a group, they greatly strengthen their home economies and infuse the Nordic region with an infectious can-do spirit.

A coherent sense of direction

Early in this chapter, we explored two critical attributes of Nordic con-sciousness: a *sense of limits* concerning Nature's biological carrying capacity and human endurance plus an adaptive capacity to *sense opportunity*. Both qualities arise from a spiritual intelligence that links Nordic people to

Nature and the needs of future generations, thereby creating a *strategic sense of direction*. This perceptive capacity catalyzes Nordic leadership in renewable energy, biotechnology and circular economy solutions plus the growth of BINC technologies, which enable Nordic companies to partner with Nature.

These higher thinking capacities also enable Nordic economies to look beyond the traditional boundaries of government and private enterprise to find creative solutions that optimize systemic wellbeing with the least amount of financial, ecological and social risk. Because Nordic people trust this system of public–private collaboration, they have become more engaged, innovative and capable of accessing their higher thinking capacities. In doing so, they have created an adaptive system with multiple feedback loops that continually refresh the system from within.

The ubiquity of such collaborations and feedback loops in Nordic economies has created what Harvard Professor Michael Porter calls "strategic clusters." Like Kalundborg, these are hotbeds of idea sharing and entrepreneurship that increase productivity, drive innovation and stimulate new business. According to Porter, when such clusters reach a critical threshold, they create significant competitive advantages in world markets – a condition affirmed by the number and type of Nordic companies annually listed in the Global 100.

Noting these dynamics, Joseph Stiglitz, a 2001 Nobel Laureate in economics, today advocates a "third way" philosophy where governments and the free market work together to generate outcomes better than either can produce alone. Observing how each can complement the other, he does not advocate a formulaic approach but recognizes that the balance will differ from time to time and place to place (much the way a complex ecosystem adapts). As former chairman of the US Council of Economic Advisors (1995–7), later named by *Time* magazine (2011) as one of the 100 most influential people in the world, Stiglitz has long admired the Nordic Model and its egalitarian values.

The reasons for this are not hard to discern. Through public–private partnerships, Nordic countries have achieved multiple wins: spreading wealth through the region by growing local networks (suppliers, partners, etc.), creating jobs, supporting government safety nets and generating investment returns. The wealth-producing partnership achieved by the government of Finland and Neste is an excellent example. Norway's $1.1

trillion sovereign wealth fund, fed by its two-thirds ownership of Equinor, is another. So too is the formation of Iceland's new sovereign wealth fund supported by dividends and resource rents from its national power company (Landsvirkjun).

Observing such synergies, Stiglitz comments: "We wrote the rules once before to make the economy more unequal, and now we have to rewrite them once again to make them more equal."

> Even if it is granted that the United States is the leader and Scandinavia are followers, there are theoretical grounds for arguing that the Nordic model may in fact be better for innovation, suggesting that if the US adopted some of the Nordic institutions, innovations would be higher, and societal welfare would be improved even more.
>
> Joseph Stiglitz, Nobel Laureate in Economics, 2014[13]

Notes

1 Lene Rachel Andersen and Marion Chertow. 2016. "Kalundborg at 40: adaptation and evolution." pp. 25–29. "Next Scandinavia – meaningful growth." Available from: https://www.nextscandinavia.com [Accessed June 29, 2020].
2 M Kettunen et al. 2012. "Socio-economic importance of ecosystem services in the Nordic countries – synthesis in the context of the economics of ecosystems and biodiversity (TEEB)," Nordic Council of Ministers. Available from: http://img.teebweb.org/wp-content/uploads/2013/01/TEEB-Nordic-Synthesis-Report.pdf [Accessed June 29, 2020].
3 The evolution of Kalundborg's Symbiosis was uniquely the result of bottom-up citizen engagement rather than top-down government directive. See: Green Exchange, Kalundborg-Symbiosis-40th-anniversary-publication pdf
4 Robert H Nelson. 2017. *Lutheranism and the Nordic Spirit of Social Democracy: A Different Protestant Ethic.* Aarhus, Denmark.
5 Extracted from Nordic Council of Ministers website (April 2019). Available from: https://www.norden.org/en/nordic-solutions-global-challenges [Accessed June 29, 2020].
6 The Good Country Index. https://www.goodcountry.org/index/results
7 Neste Annual Report 2017, p. 6. Available from: http://ir-service.funkton.com/download/ahBzfmlyLXNlcnZpY2UtaHJkchsLEg5GaWxlQXRoYWNobWVudBiAgNDklbiKCAw/Neste_Annual Report_2017.pdf?action=open

8   Neste Sustainability Report 2018, p. 5. Available from: https://www.neste.com/corporate-info/sustainability/climate-and-resource-efficiency/our-impact-climate

9   Novo Holdings A/S 2019 Annual Report, p. 1. Available from: https://www.novoholdings.dk/news/novo-holdings-annual-report-2018/

10 Nordic Bildung. 2018. "Creating new models for society." Available from: http://nordicbildung.org/

11 Lene Rachel Andersen and Stehen Rasmussen. 2015. "How will tomorrow's technologies change our societies?" *The World Economic Forum.* February 12. Available from: https://www.weforum.org/agenda/2015/02/how-will-tomorrows-technologies-change-our-societies-2

12 Bhaskar Chakravorti et al. "Digital planet 2017: how competitiveness and trust in digital economies vary across the world," The Fletcher School, Tufts University. July 2017. Available from: https://sites.tufts.edu/digitalplanet/files/2020/03/Digital_Planet_2017_FINAL.pdf

13 Joseph E Stiglitz. 2014. "Leaders and followers: perspectives on the nordic model and the economics of innovation," September 2014. Available from: https://www.nber.org/papers/w20493

8

THE NORDIC RENAISSANCE

The economic imperatives of our time call for an evolution of our consciousness from an ego-based system to an eco-based system, from one
state of awareness to another.

C. Otto Scharmer[1]

Nature underlines the very functioning of our socio-economic systems.
Nordic Council of Ministers[2]

The extraordinary success of Nordic life-mimicking economies reveals
an emerging renaissance. Beyond generating the world's highest standards of living, Nordic countries also produce a disproportionate share of
the world's most innovative publicly traded corporations. The common
denominator in the success of these companies, as with Nordic economic
thinking, is a mindset that places a higher value on living assets (people
and Nature) than on non-living capital assets – a practical ideal that reverses
the priorities of industrial capitalism.

This paradigm shift in thinking is the heart of the Nordic Renaissance.
Rather than believing humanity to be the legitimate owner/manager of

Nature (an ego-centric concept), the life-mimicking Nordic Model perceives humanity as an interdependent part of Nature (an eco-centric concept).

As leaders of this cultural renaissance, Nordic countries approach economies as sub-systems of Nature rather than super-systems that are above Nature. Similar to the earlier European Renaissance, this radical shift in awareness is validated by advances in science and human development as well as practical experience.

Nordic skills in systems thinking, for example, are affirmed by the new sciences of relativity (the idea that everything in the universe is moving relative to everything else) and chaos theory (what happens when complex systems are pushed beyond their limits). As a model for understanding life, this mental framework is fundamentally different from the older industrial paradigm of mechanistic, linear thinking that emerged from 17th-century Newtonian science.

In the related fields of cognition and human development, Nordic countries approach learning as a life-long pursuit of self-development (Bildung) that enables people to modify their thinking as their consciousness expands beyond the self to the larger living world and future generations. In keeping with this ideal, Peter Kemp, a renowned Danish educator/philosopher, urges Nordic people to become citizens of the world: to think beyond national interests "without necessarily abrogating them" and to take greater responsibility for the future of the world.[3]

In reaching for transformative global solutions, however impractical they may seem in today's inward-looking political economies, Kemp's ideal resonates in Nordic countries, where cultural norms of multiple-loop learning and expanded circles of belonging have put them on the cutting edge of change. Cogent examples of this holistic sense of responsibility include the region's many contributions to the UN's 2030 Sustainable Development Goals and the technology advances of Nordic companies in the fields of renewable energy and energy-saving cleantech, where they have become world leaders.

Energy as strategic game changer

Because energy is involved in virtually every facet of a modern economy, there is nothing more important to get right. If a country or region has sufficient energy to meet its economic requirements, virtually anything is possible. If not, economies become increasingly vulnerable no matter how powerful they once were. For this reason, energy is often called the world's master resource.

In the half-century between 1970 and 2020, the Nordic region became acutely aware of the risks of fossil fuel dependence. This started with the tenfold price increase for oil between 1970 and 1980. It was later amplified by the accumulating damage to global ecosystems from toxic waste and climate change. A further concern was the centralization of power in countries with large fossil fuel industries, which contravened Nordic egalitarian, democratic traditions.

To redress these problems, Nordic governments began in the early 1990s to aggressively tax carbon fuels. By slowing the rate at which fossil fuels were consumed and creating space for renewables to become cost-competitive, these taxes became a strategic game changer. As a result, by 2017, roughly two-thirds of the Nordic region's electricity was generated from renewables – a stark contrast to the rest of the world, which derives two-thirds of its generated power from fossil fuels.

Another important development of this period was Norway's creation in 1990 of a sovereign wealth fund for the benefit of all its people. Funded by the rent and earnings from its large offshore oil/gas reserves, it had a 2019 market valuation of roughly $1.1 trillion (more than double Norway's $435 billion gross domestic product (GDP) at the time). Considered as an economic buffer, the fund offers both citizens and the government space to think broadly about Norway's future and its role as an exemplary global change agent.

A wonderful example of this is how Equinor, Norway's giant oil company, which is two-thirds owned by the Norwegian government, became a global leader in carbon capture and storage (CCS) technology.[4] Using data obtained from its offshore Sleipner CCS plant, which has operated since 1996, Equinor provides critical insights into the effects of underground carbon storage over long periods of time. Data collected from Sleipner are now regularly published by the CO_2 Data Share Consortium led by the Norwegian research organization SINTEF to help researchers across the world understand the technology and develop safer methods for carbon dioxide (CO_2) storage.[5]

Nordic Edge, another such futuristic thinking center, is a nonprofit smart city accelerator with a global following. Founded in 2015 with a goal of making cities "smart with a heart," it aims to create "urban spaces where citizen interests and well-being come first" – conditions enabled by Nordic advances in clean energy, smart grids and digital technologies. In keeping with Peter Kemp's "Citizen of the World" vision, Nordic Edge inspired the creation of the Nordic Smart City Network in 2018/19, a collaboration of 20 cities supported by a joint Nordic Urban Living Lab that explores best practices in areas of common interest. Together, both organizations promote smart city solutions to urban centers around the world based on Nordic experience and know-how.

The development of such active multidisciplinary networks naturally generates multiplier effects: digital hubs that lower the costs of electricity and power distribution via regional smart grid networks – infrastructures that advance the development of the futuristic BINC technologies described in Chapter Seven. Commenting on such multipliers, a 2016 report by the International Renewable Energy Agency (IRENA) projected that renewable energy systems, combined with digitalization and smart data, had the potential to accelerate global GDP growth by as much as $1.3 trillion by 2030 – indicating a significant return on investment.[6]

To expand the generative power of such investment, the Nordic Council of Ministers' Working Group for Renewable Energy promotes Nordic technology and know-how to world markets as a practical means of attaining the UN's 2030 Sustainable Development Goals and generating regional export earnings: a win-win for the region and the world.

> The Working Group for Renewable Energy is charged with helping and supporting the Nordic countries' political and professional work in renewable energy by exchanging information and setting up co-operation projects between the countries. In addition, the group will market Nordic technology and know-how on renewable energy to neighboring countries, to the EU and globally.
>
> The Nordic Council of Ministers[7]

Corporate leaders in renewables

To illuminate the value added by Nordic contributions to the field of renewable energy, it is interesting to see the diversity of the region's offerings.

This we will do by reviewing six leadership companies, some of which have already been discussed, then assessing their shareholder returns relative to those of Exxon/Mobil, which has long been regarded as the world's most prominent fossil fuel company.

The first of these Nordic leaders, Fortum, is a diversified holding company based in Finland, which provides communities with low-carbon energy solutions and smart power grids using, whenever possible, local resources and renewable fuels derived from recycled waste. Fortum's energy offers cover a broad range including wind, solar, hydro, biomass, recycling and resource recovery systems, combined heat and power (CHP) systems and energy storage systems that support local power grids. With such a wide range of offers, Fortum can improve resource and energy efficiency in diverse areas – from the advanced markets of Scandinavia to less developed ones in India and Africa. Although a mid-sized company with 2019 revenues of €5.45 billion ($6.1 billion), it has become a world leader in circular economy innovations and clean, renewable energy.

In addition to Fortum, two Danish companies stand out: Vestas, the world's largest and fastest-growing producer of wind turbine generators and Ørsted, the world's largest developer of offshore windfarms. Often working in partnership, their most efficient systems can now produce electricity at half the cost of natural gas.

In the fast-growing field of transportation fuels, Nordic companies now produce high-performance biodiesel and aviation fuel from biowaste using enzymes produced by Novozymes. Leading companies in this sector include UPM-Kymenne, a forest products company that engineered the world's first commercial-scale plant for producing wood-based biodiesel and naphtha; Neste, whose biorefineries in Finland, Holland and Singapore produce diesel and jet fuels from waste fat, vegetable oil and other food-based residues; and Inbicon (an Ørsted subsidiary), which converts waste wheat straw into cellulosic ethanol for transportation fuel plus electricity and district heat.

At a time when the global economy is virtually drowning in toxic, climate-altering carbon emissions, it is hard to overstate the importance of these Nordic companies and their renewable energy technologies. Given the increasingly high costs of extracting fossil fuels from the Earth plus the economic costs of remediating the damage they do to the biosphere and human health, renewable energy has become a global growth industry with immense potential for sustainable development and future innovation.

As world markets awaken to these realities, Nordic leaders in renewable energy production have become financial front-runners. For the decade through yearend 2019, their total shareholder returns (which includes dividends) were significantly stronger than those of Exxon/Mobil, as shown in Table 8.1.

The performance disparities shown here convey both the strength and pioneering spirit of the emerging Nordic Renaissance. Instead of developing technologies to conquer Nature by drilling for oil and gas in increasingly difficult areas, Nordic renewable energy companies use their advanced technical skills to partner with Nature. As their technical expertise has grown in this field, so have their shareholder returns compared to fossil fuel companies. This is particularly true of Vestas (Chapter Six), whose upward trajectory began in 2013 – shortly after its system-monitoring super computer system came online. Due to the timing of this event, Vestas' one-to five-year returns are more compelling than its ten-year results.

Table 8.1 Nordic Clean Energy Leaders versus S&P Global Oil Index

Company	World Leadership Category	% Total Return Through Yearend 2019			
		1 Year	3 Years	5 Years	10 Years
Fortum	Clean energy holding company	24.18	82.97	71.81	177.3
Neste	Biofuel from organic waste	44.14	281.31	548.03	1,099.34
Novozymes	Enzymes for making biofuels	13.87	27.12	16.46	344.0
Ørsted	Offshore windfarms	58.90	253.36	NMF	NMF
UPM	Biofuel from wood	27.12	41.57	255.70	405.0
Vestas	Manufacturer of windmills	29.15	146.04	266.63	134.4
Average Share Price Performance		**32.89**	**138.73**	**231.73**	**43**
Exxon/Mobil Largest US oil company		−8.65	−2.55	0.42	41.68

Note: Total shareholder returns for the decade ending 2019.
NMF means Ørsted had no publicly traded shares for the period under consideration.

Energy return on investment

One of the best indicators of energy value is a metric called energy return on investment (EROI). This is defined as the amount of energy delivered from a particular resource in relation to the amount of energy used to obtain and manage that resource over its projected lifetime. High ratios naturally attract investors because they generate high "net energy" yields and hence high return on shareholder investment.

The poor performance of Exxon/Mobil, as shown in Table 8.1, reflects the rising costs of finding new oil as the world's best reserves become depleted. The same holds true for the 1,400 companies in the S&P Global Oil Index, whose aggregate investment performance significantly lagged that of Exxon/Mobil over the period shown.

According to University of Turin scholar Joseph Bonauiti, the EROI on global fossil fuels peaked in the 1930s and has been declining ever since, save for improvements in technology that enabled brief EROI recoveries. As a result, he says advanced capitalist societies have entered a phase of declining marginal returns – or *involuntary de-growth* – with deleterious effects on their "institutional framework" of fossil fuel dependent industries.[8]

By contrast, we find high and rising EROIs on wind energy compared to those of fossil fuels, nuclear energy and hydropower. This trend was initially noted in a 2009 study titled "Meta-Analysis of Net Energy Return for Wind Power Systems." Published in Elsevier's journal, *Renewable Energy*, the study compared the amount of primary energy used in the building, operation and decommissioning of energy systems compared to their lifetime energy output – a protocol designed to address all stages of an energy system.[9] Although the data generated by this study have been superseded, its conclusions are more valid today than when the article was written because the EROI on wind power has significantly increased while those on fossil fuels and nuclear power have decreased.

For the record, the 2009 meta-analysis was based on data from 119 wind turbines operating between 1997 and 2007 – a time when older wind turbines had EROIs of 19.8 and newer ones of 25.2. By comparison, the EROI on coal at the time was 8.0 and that on nuclear energy was in the vicinity of 9.1 (although this varied widely depending on assumptions about the disposal of spent fuels).

Today's giant wind turbines have significantly higher EROIs because of their access to higher wind currents. Although they cost more to build, the electricity output over their working lives more than justifies the extra expense. According to a 2020 website posting on Vestas Tall Turbines, "A modern wind turbine produces almost twice as much electricity compared to one built just 10 years ago."[10] Because Vestas' technology is continuously improving, this record is likely to be eclipsed.

> Although larger turbines require greater initial energy investments in materials, the increase in power output due to improvements more than compensates for this over the lifetime of the turbine ... Another reason larger turbines have a larger EROI is the well-known "cube rule" of wind power, i.e. the power available from the wind varies as the cube of the wind speed.
>
> Kubiszewski et al.[11]

For purposes of comparison, a 2018 study of the world's 30 largest oil companies titled "A New Approach to Calculating the 'Corporate' EROI," determined that the EROIs for many of the world's largest integrated energy companies (including BP, Chevron, Exxon/Mobil, Shell and Total) were ten or lower,[12] which puts them at a significant disadvantage to wind-generated electricity.

An earlier (2014) paper titled "EROI of different fuels and their implications for society" published in Elsevier's journal, Energy Policy, puts this comparatively low EROI in context. According to its lead author, Charles AS Hall, the decline in energy company returns is due to the depletion of older oil and gas reserves, which led to the authors' conclusion: "[W]hile there remains considerable energy in the ground it is unlikely to be exploitable cheaply, or eventually at all, because of its decreasing EROI."[13]

Consequently, while massive amounts of oil and gas remain embedded in the world's giant shale deposits, the average EROIs on these reserves are often below company breakeven points. Because of this deficiency, there has been a rising trend of bankruptcies among US shale developers. According to a January 2020 report by Oilprice.com, between 2015 and November 2019, more than 200 shale companies declared bankruptcy involving a combined $121.7 billion in debt.[14]

By contrast, the Nordic renewable energy companies listed in Table 8.1 have widened their EROI advantages due to technology advances and increasing economies of scale. For example, between the time Vestas brought its Firestorm supercomputer online in June 2011 and yearend 2019, the EROI on its largest wind turbines has risen sharply.

The efficiencies of waste-to-energy plants are also compelling, as Neste's strong shareholder returns attest, because they generate revenue both when they accept waste (via tipping fees) and when they sell their biofuels. Consequently, their operating costs reside mainly in the construction and maintenance of their facilities plus administrative overhead.

The same cost/benefit variables apply to Sweden's 34 waste-to-energy plants, many of which are operated by Fortum. By converting waste into electricity and district heat, these low-carbon-emitting plants reduce Sweden's need for fuel oil imports by roughly 500,000 metric tons per year.

What we find in this data is a transformative multiple-win proposition that stands in stark contrast to the declining effectiveness of fossil fuels. Just as the European Renaissance marked a turning point in human history, we see similar patterns today in the Nordic world – particularly in their approach to energy.

As mentioned earlier, Nordic advances in renewable energy are complemented by their technology leadership in "cleantech." Prominent leaders in this field include two previously described Nordic Global 100 companies: Atlas Copco (energy saving) and Tomra (recycling, resource recovery). As mentioned in Chapter Four, their shares have been strong since the turn of the millennium. Interestingly, the strongest period of such growth was the decade ending in 2019 – a time when world economies began to seriously reckon with their over-dependence on fossil fuels and depleting Earth's resources. During that ten-year period, the shares of Atlas Copco and Tomra generated total returns of 928% and 802%, respectively.

Beyond contributing to the health of their home economies, the greatest contribution of these two cleantech exemplars may be the impact of their success on Nordic startups. We find evidence of this in the spectacular growth of the annual Nordic Cleantech Open: a competition for entrepreneurs from the Nordic and Baltic regions, whose purpose is to advance circular economy technologies, which demonstrably lower their ecological footprints. The goal of the competition is to select, with the help of an international jury of investors and corporate managers, the region's 25 best seed-stage cleantech startups.

According to Cleantech Scandinavia, which initiated the open in 2010, the competition has led to the development of roughly 600 Nordic clean-tech startups. With a qualified audience of venture funds, multinational companies, cities, consultants and government organizations, the event adds to the image and momentum of Nordic leadership in this transforma-tive economic field.

The popularity of this and similar startup events also reflects the prag-matism of the Nordic Model, which dynamically blends idealism (lowering humanity's ecological footprint) with free market capitalism. Consequently, what started out as a series of circular economy experiments in Kalundborg in the 1970s has become a popular regional quest – a desire that reaches across generations and public–private boundaries toward creating more harmonious relationships between civilization and Nature.

From a cultural perspective, this quest is rooted in the Nordic philoso-phy of education (Bildung) whose processes and goals reinforce a sense of responsibility to the health of the whole system (Nature and society). This shared commitment, as demonstrated in Appendix One, is a compelling source of organizational leverage (trust, open inspired networking), which generates technological leverage (renewable energy, biotechnology, clean-tech, etc.) and ultimately, market leverage (favorable terms of trade).

Culture is an instrument for growth, as shown by many years of Nordic success in the area... The historically strong bond between the Nordic people and nature ... permeates culture but also the relationship to nature itself. In an interplay between culture, nature, and social responsibility, we strive to successfully manage our heritage. The common responsibil-ity for natural and human resources permeates decision-making in both business and politics.

Nordic Council of Ministers, 2018[15]

Inclusiveness as catalyst to economic development

One of the enduring strengths of Nordic innovation is its inclusiveness. Because of the region's open egalitarian, democratic culture, everyone has a stake in the system. And everyone has an equal voice. This ethos, as shown throughout this book, supports a robust spirit of continuous learn-ing, networking and civic engagement that amplifies systems thinking and economic results by engaging all people, instead of favoring the few at the top. Recognizing the importance of this spirit, the World Economic Forum (WEF) asserts: "[N]o bigger policy challenge preoccupies leaders than *expanding social participation* in the process and benefits of economic growth."[16]

This statement implicitly recognizes a core strength of life-mimicking economies: where the health of the whole supports the health of its living parts and vice versa. Even though that should be self-evident, it is not how most economies operate today. Yet the truth is right there before us. Nordic economies are prosperous precisely because they inclusively care for the health, education and well-being of all their people, including refugee immigrants.

This is validated by the World Economic Forum's global Inclusive Development Index (IDI). Launched in 2017 as part of its "System Initiative on Shaping the Future of Economic Progress," the index ranks countries' economic performance on three pillars: "growth and development, inclusion, and intergenerational equity and sustainability." Categories of inclusiveness cover access to health care, education, credit, employment, home ownership, business ownership and basic services.

Similar to other surveys mentioned in this book, Nordic countries were again clustered in the top decile of the first two IDI publications (2017; 2018). Out of 109 countries evaluated for 2017, Norway was ranked first, followed by Iceland fourth, Denmark fifth, Sweden sixth and Finland eleventh. For 2018, rankings were virtually the same, except Iceland moved up from fourth to second. By comparison, the world's seven largest advanced economies had significantly lower ratings. Of these, Germany came closest to the Nordics with a rating of 13th in 2017 and 12th in 2018. The two largest G7 countries, however, were further back in both surveys with the US at 23rd and Japan 24th. Among the world's emerging economies, China was rated 26th with lower composite scores than the US and Japan.[17,18]

The Inclusive Development Index was replaced in 2020 with a Global Social Mobility Index, which the WEF created to "show how economies benefit from fixing inequality" by offering equal opportunity to people regardless of "socio-economic status at birth." By these standards, Denmark was ranked first, followed by Norway second, Finland third, Sweden fourth and Iceland fifth – a strong validation of their egalitarian democracies, free education systems and shared economic development strategies. Among the world's largest developed economies, Germany (11th) again came closest to the Nordics while the US (27th) dropped further back.[19]

As further evidence of Nordic inclusiveness and the paradigm shift taking place in their life-mimicking political-economic systems, at yearend 2019, the prime ministers of Denmark, Finland, Norway and Iceland were all women. In addition, Sweden claims to have the world's "first feminist government."[20] All of these outcomes reflect the high value women place on inclusiveness, holistic thinking, co-operation, transparent communication, social trust and maintaining healthy living conditions, and the desire of Nordic citizens to maintain these values. In accordance with the Global Social Mobility Index, this reflects a growing awareness among Nordic citizens that the foregoing qualities are essential foundations of their economic health.

Another factor in the rise of women as Nordic political-economic leaders is the failing performance of countries governed by privileged elites (most of whom are men) – especially their tendencies to marginalize labor and underfund essential social services. Over time, as we see in the current struggles of countries operating under the neoclassical model, such neglect becomes a systems trap in which hardship feeds on itself: where productivity and tax revenues cannot keep up with the costs of maintaining even minimum levels of health, education and welfare and where the very neglect of human capital feeds back to weaken economic resilience.

This anomaly explains why the US, in spite of its vast resources, markets and advanced technology, is currently locked in a self-reinforcing cycle of fiscal deficits. While some believe artificial intelligence and automation technologies will eventually mitigate these adverse feedbacks, if all they do is replace workers with capital assets that further reduce inclusiveness and widen the gap between rich and poor, the application of such technologies will only make matters worse.

Understanding such realities, Nordic countries have resolutely chosen a path of labor-friendly "sharing economies."[21] In a world that is increasingly overcrowded and resource constrained, this requires leaders who think broadly about the health of the whole rather than the narrow self-interests of a select few – women and men committed to promoting full domestic employment while also advancing the UN's Sustainable Development Goals in the global markets they serve.

Considered in this context, inclusiveness does more than provide Nordic citizens with a high common standard of living. Because Nordic people are culturally inclined to think holistically, they understand that their economic well-being is ultimately connected to the health of the global system in which they exist. More than any advanced technical skill, this awareness is the secret to their economic success and the source of their political-economic renaissance.

A more robust model of capitalism

Because Nordic economies place such a high value on inclusiveness, critics of their system often call them "socialist" or soft. In the US, such criticisms are often accompanied by warnings that countries following the Nordic Model will end up like Russia, Cuba, Venezuela or North Korea, whose centrally controlled economies perform far below their potential.

This is nonsense. The Nordics, whose combined population is less than a fifth of Russia's, produced in 2019 a roughly equivalent GDP ($1.63 trillion versus $1.66 trillion). When stated on a GDP per capita basis, the average result for the Nordic region was $59,400 compared to $11,290 for Russia. Even when adjusted for purchase price parity (PPP), Nordic results are far ahead.

As mentioned in Chapter Two, all five Nordic countries have been rated higher than the US on the Legatum Prosperity Index. In addition, their citizens are healthier, happier and live longer than their US peers, thanks to universal free education and health care and the confidence of knowing their pensions are fully funded. Consequently, partisan US rhetoric about the Nordic region being "a road to ruin" is, in fact, a more apt description of their own economic model.

Indeed, when compared side-by-side, the Nordic Model embraces the best qualities of capitalism (free markets, globalization, private property rights and democracy) while protecting citizens against some of its riskier attributes (massive wealth gaps plus unequal access to health, education and welfare). The net result of these policies is a dynamic system that optimizes human potential and income equality, which the World Economic Forum considers essential for sustainable economic progress. To most Nordic citizens, the cost of this system (high individual tax rates) is a reasonable price to pay for the benefits it bestows.

Interestingly, as the Nordic Renaissance progresses, we now hear opinion leaders within the neoclassical stronghold of Wall Street praising its advantages. For example, Michael Cembalest, chairman of market and investment strategy at JP Morgan Asset Management (a mainstay of US capitalist enterprise) devoted a significant part of his June 2019 "Eye on the Market" commentary to a comparison of Nordic business conditions relative to those in the US. Supported by diverse charts and data, he affirmed that the Nordic Model is, in many ways, freer than the US model.

> Nordic countries rank higher than the US with respect to "Business Freedoms", which include streamlined regulations for new businesses creation, and the ease and cost of obtaining licenses and real estate development permits. Nordic countries are also more open to free trade than the US (this was true even before Trump's tariff barriers), are more open to foreign direct investment and apply fewer capital controls. Nordics are also very protective of physical and intellectual property rights, and the adverse impact of Nordic government regulation on competition is lower than in the US.
>
> Michael Cembalest, JP Morgan Asset Management, 2019[22]

Although Cembalest did not comment on the political-economic philosophies underlying the two systems, it is clear to objective onlookers that key elements of the Nordic system (capitalism and universal care) effectively reinforce one another. By enabling people to realize their potential as intelligent creative individuals, the system generates some of the world's highest labor participation rates and per capita productivity.

The reason for this is simple. As shown throughout this book, management by means (MBM) strategies, which focus on the well-being of people and Nature (the means of economic value creation), regularly outperform the more self-serving management by results (MBR) strategies of countries operating on the neoclassical model. Such inclusive strategies are, in fact, the beating heart of the Nordic Renaissance.

In light of these realities, political-economic leaders who call the Nordic Model "socialist" appear to be more concerned about losing their power and privilege than about sustainable economic progress. This is particularly true of politicians and executives wedded to the fossil fuel and related industries (autos, finance, chemicals, pharmaceuticals), whose models of success are now threatened or collapsing under the weight of climate change, ecosystem degradation, compounding debt and social divisiveness.

Economics does not have to be about exploiting people and Nature. As revealed throughout this book, we now see a better way forward grounded in living and working harmoniously with all life. To achieve such harmony, political-economic cultures must develop a broad understanding that societies and economies are sub-systems of Nature, not super-systems that are above Nature, and that we humans are one of many species whose survival depends on living symbiotically with the whole biospheric web of life.

This knowledge is powerfully disruptive. Today, as our lives become more challenged by world population growth and the destruction of essential ecosystems that feed and shelter us, we are now forced to ask: What is the purpose of economics? Is it to serve a privileged few at the expense of Nature and the general public? Or is it to elevate the whole by serving all of its living parts (people and Nature)? We have a choice.

Notes

1 C Otto Scharmer. 2013. "From ego-system to eco-system economies," *Open Democracy*. September 23. Available from: https://www.opendemocracy.net/en/transformation/from-ego-system-to-eco-system-economies/ [Accessed June 29, 2020].

2 Nordic Council of Ministers. "Socio-economic importance of ecosystem services in the Nordic countries," *TEEB Nordic Synthesis Report*, p. 16. Available from: http://dx.doi.org/10.6027/TN2012-559.

3 Peter Kemp. 2011. *Citizen of the World: The Cosmopolitan Ideal for the Twenty-First Century*. Amherst, NY: Humanity Books.

4 Equinor. 2019. *Sleipner Partnership Releases CO2 Storage Data*. Available from: https://www.equinor.com/en/news/2019-06-12-sleipner-co2-storage-data.html

5 SINTEF. 2019. *Sleipner Partnership Releases CO2 Storage Data*. Available from: https://www.sintef.no/en/latest-news/sleipner-partnership-releases-co2-storage-data/

6 International Renewable Energy Agency (IRENA). 2016. *Renewable Energy Benefits: Measuring the Economics*. January 2016. Available from: https://www.irena.org/DocumentDownloads/Publications/IRENA_Measuring-the-Economics_2016.pdf

7 https://www.norden.org/en/organisation/working-group-renewable-energy

8 Joseph Bonauiti. 2018. "Are we entering the age of involuntary degrowth?" *Journal of Cleaner Production*. 1(Part 2): pp. 1800–9.

9 Ida Kubiszewski et al. 2010. "Meta-analysis of net energy return for wind power systems," *Renewable Energy*. 35(1): pp. 218–25. Available from: https://www.researchgate.net/publication/222703134_Meta-Analysis_of _Net_Energy_Return_for_Wind_Power_Systems [Accessed June 29, 2020].

10 Vestas. *Tall Turbines Unlocking the Cheapest Source of Power*. Available from: https://www.vestas.com/en/about/discover_wind/tallturbines#!

11 Op. cit. Kubiszewski et al., "Meta-analysis of net energy return for wind power systems," p. 3.

12 L Celi et al. 2018. "A new approach to calculating the 'corporate' EROI," *BioPhysical Economics and Resource Quality*. 3(article 15). Available from: https://link.springer.com/article/10.1007/s41247-018-0048-1#citeas

13 Charles AS Hall et al. 2014. "EROI of different fuels and their implications for society," *Energy Policy*. 64(January): pp. 141–52. Available from: https://www.sciencedirect.com/science/article/pii/S0301421513003856

14 Nick Cunningham. 2020. "U.S. Shale patch sees huge jump in bankrupt-cies," OilPrice.com. January 23. Available from: https://oilprice.com/Energy/Energy-General/US-Shale-Patch-Sees-Huge-Jump-In-Bankruptcies.html

15 Norden. The Nordic Perspective. "Strategy for international branding of the Nordic region 2015–2018," p. 18. Available from: http://norden.diva-portal.org/smash/get/diva2:783406/FULLTEXT01.pdf [Accessed June 29, 2020].

16 The World Economic Forum. "The inclusive growth and development report 2017." Geneva 2017. Available from: https://www.weforum.org/reports/the-inclusive-growth-and-development-report-2017

17 The World Economic Forum. "The inclusive devlopment index (IDI)." Table 1. Geneva 2017. Available from: http://reports.weforum.org/inclusive-growth-and-development-report-2017/tables-1-to-16/

18 The World Economic Forum. "The inclusive development index 2018: summary and data highlights." Available from: http://www3.weforum.org/docs/WEF_Forum_IncGrwth_2018.pdf

19 The World Economic Forum. "The social mobility report 2020." Available from: http://reports.weforum.org/social-mobility-report-2020/social-mobility-rankings/

20 Government Offices of Sweden. "A feminist government." March 8, 2020. Available from: https://www.government.se/government-policy/a-feminist-government/

21 Nordic Council of Ministers. TemaNord 2018:516. "Nordic labour markets and the sharing economy." Available from: http://norden.diva-portal.org/smash/get/diva2:1182946/FULLTEXT01.pdf [Accessed June 29, 2020].

22 Michael Cembalest. 2019. "Eye on the market" J.P. Morgan Asset Management. June 24. Available from: https://www.jpmorgan.com/jpmpdf/1320747403290.pdf

9

WHAT WE CAN LEARN FROM THE NORDIC MODEL

Whatever improves the circumstances of the greater part can never be regarded as an inconvenience to the whole. No society can surely be flourishing and happy, of which the far greater part of the members are poor and miserable.

Adam Smith, *The Wealth of Nations*[1]

Our peaceful, democratic and inclusive societies, where everybody participates and has rights and responsibilities, are strong societies that can cope with even the biggest of challenges.

Nordic Council of Ministers: *Our Vision 2030*[2]

The world has reached a tipping point. As populations everywhere awaken to the tragedies of climate change, ecosystem degradation, crushing debt, social divisiveness and the collective impact of these failures on public well-being, people have begun to push back against the increasingly self-destructive neoclassical model of political-economy. In the midst of this breakdown, business and government leaders have begun to see the life-mimicking Nordic Model as a sustainable *breakthrough*. Significantly, this shift in perception recalls Adam Smith's ideal that good governance fundamentally looks to the wellbeing of the whole.

Widely recognized as the father of economics and modern capitalism, Smith did not advocate completely free markets, as some suppose. Although he passionately believed in markets, he cautioned that they could become inefficient if power became concentrated in too few hands. Absent free and open competition, he reasoned, companies would be tempted to exploit workers and customers because: "The interest of dealers ... in any particular branch of trade or manufactures, is always in some respect different, and even opposite to, that of the public."

Another commonly held belief about Smith is that he advocated for individual self-interest and economic liberty – a self-centered approach that puts the interests of business owners above all else. But that too is a misreading. In the first sentence of his book, *The Theory of Moral Sentiments*, he notes that we humans have an inbred sense of caring: "However selfish man may be," he wrote, "there are evidently some principles in his nature, which interest him in the fortune of others, and render their happiness necessary to him, though he derives nothing from it except the pleasure of seeing it."[3]

The ethical components of Smith's political-economic philosophy are generally lost on neoclassical economists and most business leaders, whose holy grail is growth of gross domestic product (GDP) and profit. As shown throughout this book, their ego-centric thinking, where ends too often justify unethical means, puts both society and Nature at risk. By placing a higher value on non-living capital assets than on living assets (people and Nature), which are the essential source of our economic wellbeing, such "leaders" corrupt and degrade the entire system.

Smith understood this. Reflecting on the negative feedback of exploitive business practices, including price gouging, he observed in *The Wealth of Nations*: "The rate of profit ... is always highest in the countries which are going fastest to ruin." In other words, when power becomes too centralized in the hands of a few, who exploit their pricing power to the detriment of the general public, social and economic conditions suffer.

England's Corn Laws (1815–1846) were a good example of this. By imposing tariffs on imported grain to protect the revenues of a landed aristocracy – many of whom were members of parliament – they raised the price of food staples for the urban working class, who had to spend the bulk of their income on grain just to survive. Since that left most people with little income for other purchases, they could not afford manufactured products, which meant manufacturers had to lay off workers. Those workers, in turn, had difficulty finding employment, so the economic spiral worsened for everyone involved. Because of this, repeal of the Corn Laws eventually became a nationwide middle-class moral crusade. Led by Richard Cobden, an entrepreneur and progressive influenced by the ideals of Adam Smith, it led to a quick economic turnaround.

After repeal of the Corn Laws, British manufacturing saw significant increases in productivity as the country moved toward freer trade policies. This was accelerated by a growing emphasis on public education with special attention given to educating the poor. These progressive policies, also championed by Cobden, greatly strengthened England's supply of human capital and its manufacturing capacity. By 1860, the country ranked as the world's largest trading nation and its middle class entered a period of rapid growth. By 1870, led by advances in technology, England entered its second industrial revolution; and by the end of the century, its middle class had grown so that only 15% of its population was classified as poor according to the UK economic statistician, Arthur L Bowley.

Considered in this context, the market is desirable not as an end in itself, or because it makes possible economic growth and private gain, but because it serves the general public and enables society as a whole to flourish. This definition of flourishing, as seen throughout this book, is a core premise of the emerging life-mimicking paradigm. By linking the health of Nordic political-economies to the health of their citizens and the natural world, these countries have become progressively more coherent and effective.

In Chapter Three, we saw how this fundamental premise of Nordic economics lifted Denmark, Sweden and Norway from being some of the poorest countries in Europe to some of the most prosperous in the space of three generations. The catalyst of this transformation was an emerging philosophy of education called folk Bildung, which instilled in people a collective sense of caring for each other and Nature. Instead of valuing individual wealth, Bildung valued individual knowledge, self-development and a sense of responsibility to the whole.

Central to this philosophy was the Smithian ideal of lifting people from poverty, which the Swiss author and educator, Johann Pestalozzi called

Burgerliche Bildung (civic *Bildung*). This sense of civic responsibility became embedded in the curricula of folk schools for young adults in Denmark, Norway and Sweden during the 1860s and continues today as the conceptual foundation of the Nordic region's universal care system.

It is hard to imagine the high quality of life and productivity in the Nordic world, or the Nordic Bioeconomy Initiative, absent this culture of mutual caring and pursuit of knowledge. As revealed by Helsinki's annual Slush events (Chapter Two), these egalitarian symbiotic values are very much alive today among a new generation of entrepreneurs committed to "take personal responsibility for the future we want to see." Although traditionally-minded skeptics may scoff at this as utopian "pie in the sky," it is in fact a purer and more robust form of capitalism than the neoclassical model. As shown throughout these pages, the Nordic Model accomplishes this by attending to the health of the whole rather than the self-serving interests of powerful elites.

Table 9.1 Comparing the effectiveness of both models

Defining Attributes Neoclassical/GDP First Model	Life-mimicking (Nordic) Model
Economies are super-systems above life	Economies as sub-systems of life
Capital is primary	Life is primary (Nature, humanity)
Focus on quantity of economic growth	Focus on quality of life (source of growth)
Management by results (GDP, profit)	Management by means (especially learning)
Unconstrained use of debt	Frugal approach to debt
Centralized political-economic power	Decentralized, democratic governance
Ego-centric linear thinking	Eco-centric, non-linear systems thinking
Limited public access to information	Open, transparent information sharing
Partial public funding of health, education	Universal access to health care, education
Intensive use of fossil fuels	Massive shift to renewable energy
Wasteful use of natural resources	Extensive recycling (circular economy)
Increasingly loose accounting practices	Disciplined (holistic) accounting practices
Political-Economic Results	
Excessive debt, unfunded liabilities	Moderate debt, healthy pension systems
Unstable social safety nets	Stable social safety nets
Increasing credit risks	Secure credit environment
Volatile monetary conditions	Resilient monetary conditions
Depleting economic resources	Efficient use of resources, renewable energy
Reduced public health	Excellent public health, high life expectancy
Wide gap between rich and poor	More even distribution of income, prosperity
Public distrust, political divisiveness	High trust, political cohesion
Decaying public morale	World's happiest people

So what can we learn from the Nordic Model in terms of its working assumptions and practices? Table 9.1 summarizes this in two parts: first, by comparing the defining attributes of the Nordic Model relative to the more mechanistic neoclassical model, then by describing how these play out in terms of political-economic results. The purpose of this summary is to show in broad conceptual terms how everything connects and why. The granular data that support this table are embodied throughout previous chapters.

When looking at the political-economic results summarized in Table 9.1, it becomes apparent that the Nordic Model contains numerous built-in buffers – secure social safety nets, stable monetary and credit conditions, efficient use of resources, more even distribution of income and prosperity and a trusting, adaptive culture – all of which enable their economies to withstand adversity and shock. The correspondingly weak social, ecological and financial conditions of the neoclassical model, by contrast, make countries operating on that model significantly more vulnerable to systemic distress and collapse.

Importance of buffers

Buffers are essential attributes of living systems because they enable individuals to survive, thrive and reproduce, thereby passing their DNA on to future generations. In human physiology, buffers include our immune system, our innate ability to sense danger and our capacity to reason. In Nature, buffers exist in the diversity of species, which strengthen the whole as they provide abundant sources of food, habitat and information. In economies, they are generated by our stewardship of the living resources we depend on for our wellbeing.

Nordic economies are effective precisely because they take a proactive, integrated approach to such stewardship – rather than treating ecological, social and financial matters as ad hoc, often competing, goals. Such integration is evident in the design of their universal safety nets, which reinforce systems thinking through their very inclusiveness and symbiotic aims. In the realm of economics, their holistic accounting systems and support of the 2030 Sustainable Development Goals reinforce the idea that it is more productive to live and work in harmony with each other, the community of nations and Nature than working in disregard or conflict.

Nordic advances in renewable energy and biotechnology are particularly strong buffers. In addition to reducing the ecological footprint of the Nordic region, they create jobs in globally competitive industries and generate profits and tax revenue, which feedback to support their universal safety nets. The region's effectiveness in such enterprise is affirmed by the large number of Nordic companies listed each year in the Global 100 of the world's most sustainable shareholder-owned companies (Appendix Two).

This feedback system itself is a super buffer because Nordic safety nets and productive enterprise reinforce one another. By providing local economies with healthy, educated, motivated workers, the system pays for itself as it develops new skills. That is also why Nordic economies have such low sovereign debt/GDP ratios and high gross national savings rates.

As the benefits of these primary buffers spread through the region, they generate new buffers within the region's prodigious startup community. This is particularly evident in its growing cleantech industry – a movement that gave rise to the popular Nordic Cleantech Open (described in Chapter Eight). We find further evidence of such activity in the extraordinary returns on the Nordic Venture Performance Index (NVPI) plus the emergence of Stockholm, Copenhagen, Helsinki and Oslo as global innovation hubs (described in Chapter Two).

Because these core and emerging elements of Nordic economies are so well integrated, they generate an upward spiral of prosperity and productivity. This capacity for continual self-renewal and development in turn strengthens the region's extraordinary social trust – a quality that generates social networking, idea sharing and a willingness to take personal responsibility for improving the quality of life. It is also a wonderful example of managing by means (MBM) because healthy people, planet and profit are the means by which countries generate and sustain prosperity.

In sum, when we compare the defining elements of the life-mimicking Nordic Model relative to those of the neoclassical/MBR model as presented in Table 9.1, it is easy to understand why the Nordic community has been so successful and why the older industrial era model is failing.

Looking at the fundamentals of both systems, it is clear which is the more promising path to the future. Although mainstream political-economists continue to look on the life-mimicking Nordic Model as a misguided experiment with radical socialism, they cannot dispute its economic results – especially in contrast to those produced by their own model.

Business leaders, on the other hand, must be more pragmatic. They cannot afford to support failing policies and practices, however entrenched these may be among mainstream political-economists. Consequently, when they see evidence of a better method, they are drawn to it. A wonderful example of this is the growing appeal of a new management approach called presencing, which replicates the ideals of the Nordic Model and its holistic philosophy of education.

Presencing: A distillation of *Bildung*

The power of the Nordic Model, as earlier stated, is the way it engages people and summons their highest (spiritual) intelligence: the intelligence that gives meaning and direction to their lives and to their creative thinking. When people authentically see themselves as part of a larger harmonic whole, they enjoy giving back and replenishing that whole, even though (as Adam Smith wrote) they derive "nothing from it except the pleasure of seeing it."

Recognizing the power of this impulse, Otto Scharmer, co-founder of MIT's Presencing Institute and chairman of the University's IDEAS program, created a process that reconnects people back to the biospheric web of life, which is our genetic and spiritual home. Called "presencing," it seeks to restore the lost connections most people feel in terms of their relationships to Nature, to each other and to themselves. The word itself integrates the words "presence" and "sensing." Similar to *Bildung*, it helps leaders (and all people) expand their capacities to empathize and connect with the world around us.

The crisis of our time isn't just a crisis of a single leader, organization, country, or conflict. The crisis manifests across all countries in the form of three major divides: the ecological divide—that is, the disconnect between self and nature; the social divide—that is, the disconnect between self and other; and the spiritual divide—that is, the disconnect between self and self.

C. Otto Scharmer[4]

As a learning discipline, presencing evolved out of MIT's Center for Organizational Learning, which was co-founded by Peter Senge and faculty colleagues together with a group of global companies in the early 1990s. The founding ideal was to foster learning in corporations, governments, schools and other institutions we rely upon as cultural and political-economic centers of influence—based on an understanding that the health of whole systems (economies, organizations, ecosystems, the human body) inexorably depends on the health of their constituent parts.

Considered as such, presencing distills the learning processes of Bildung, which aim to expand people's awareness ("circles of belonging") beyond themselves to the wellbeing of the whole (society, biosphere, future generations).

To accelerate the spread of this holistic approach to learning, Scharmer created in 2015 a free massive open online course (MOOC) based on "the art and social technology" of presencing. From its creation in 2015 to yearend 2019, the course reached over 160,000 people in 185 countries – thereby cultivating a cohort of future leaders to catalyze change as the world transitions from the neoclassical model of economy to the emerging life-mimicking one.

Although the processes of reconnecting with the living world and oneself may seem soft compared to the hard realities of corporate management, Scharmer has run coaching and leadership programs for some of the world's most powerful corporations, including Agilent Technologies, Alibaba, BASF, Daimler, Federal Express, Fujitsu, GlaxoSmithKline, Google, Hewlett Packard, McKinsey and Shell.[5,6] In addition, the Presencing Institute has an active audience in China where it conducts an innovation lab in partnership with the government "to co-facilitate high level cross sector innovation groups."[7]

The appeal of presencing to such corporate and government audiences today reflects a growing sense among leaders that traditional methods of management are failing: that they must learn to live and work in closer harmony with each other and Nature. Considered in this context, presencing validates the holistic thinking of the Nordic Model. It also conveys a shared sense of urgency that there is no time to waste: that competition for commercial and military power in an over-populated world with increasingly scarce ecological resources has become a lose-lose cycle of unacceptable risk.

COVID-19: Exposing the weakness of the neoclassical model

In the midst of this fraught situation, the world economy was confronted in November 2019 by the potentially catastrophic coronavirus pandemic. Within months it spread from China, where it was first discovered, to the rest of the world, forcing economies into precautionary slowdowns and lockdowns in order to safeguard public health. Coming at a time when the world's largest economies were struggling under the financial burdens of massive debts and unfunded liabilities, it was more than the system could bear.

All at once, the pandemic exposed the weaknesses of the neoclassical model and its inherent contradictions, which subordinate life (people and Nature) to the continual growth of GDP and profit – exploitive practices that have caused what biologists call the Earth's "sixth mass extinction" (the Anthropocene). Expanding on this theme of ecological demise, an editorial in the March 2020 *AIMS Geosciences* journal, proposed that COVID-19 could, indeed, have had human origins "due to our actions that contribute to weaken natural ecosystems."[8] While some may question whether the virus had such a derivation, the authors' larger point is well taken.

In describing this sudden calamity, Otto Scharmer observed,

> It's almost as if ... Mother Nature had suddenly sent us to our rooms to think about what we are doing to her, to each other, and to ourselves. We've been given a time-out as a species!" Which raises the critical question: "What key learnings can we take from this collective moment?"[9]

Adding to the poignancy of this catastrophic event, people everywhere have begun to see more clearly, through personal experience and social media, that we are inescapably connected to one another and Nature. Because of this, increasing numbers are awakening to the fact that how we behave as individuals and societies matters greatly to the future of the world and successive generations.

Adding to this awakening, six months after the coronavirus was first detected, the world was shocked again when an unarmed black African

American man was choked to death by a US police officer. The timing of this incident immediately struck a raw nerve – both in the US and world-wide – because it symbolized the social divides of increasingly concentrated economic power, manifest in random acts of violence against vulnerable minorities and an oligarchic disregard for life in general. For the first time in history, people took to the streets in more than 60 countries to express their collective outrage and their desires for a more equal voice in their own governance.[10]

Abetting this sudden turn of events, it was clear to many that the world economy was in a downward spiral as the fossil fuel industry tried to maintain, through political corruption, its once privileged status. More vexingly, as the energy returns on investment (EROIs) of coal, oil and natural gas declined, countries operating under the neoclassical model wasted scarce public funds by subsidizing corporate owners and lease-holders of those reserves.[11] According to *Forbes Magazine*, a US business bi-weekly, the US spent ten times more on such subsidies than on public education in 2015.[12]

Meanwhile, as the disrupting influence of this misallocation of resources fed through the US and global economies, the world's biggest investment banks covered up the decay with complex financial (hedging) strategies, including derivatives and junk bonds. However, because these treated symptoms rather than causes, the underlying problems inevitably became worse. Consequently, as unsold automobiles piled up in dealers' lots and unused commercial aircraft accumulated in "airliner boneyards," the US government was forced to issue additional multi-trillion-dollar corporate bailouts – not just for the auto, aircraft and transportation com-panies themselves, but for their suppliers and for other fossil-fuel-depend-ent sectors.

In order to fund these massive bailout operations, the US Federal Reserve and other central banks flooded world markets with trillions of dollars in new money at artificially low interest rates. This, however, further com-plicated the global misallocation of resources by disconnecting the cost of money to the critical variable of investment risk.

An additional threat to the industrial world's fossil-fuel-dependent model surfaced in April 2019 when it was disclosed in a Saudi Aramco bond prospectus that the world's largest oil/gas field (Saudi Ghawar) was pumping 25% less oil per day than had been assumed and that expensive and environmentally destructive water injection methods were being used to get that oil out of the ground.[13] This was disturbing news for two important reasons: first, because it called into question the life expectancies of the world's other large oil fields, many of which are in the volatile Middle East; and second, because it threatened the stability of this war-torn region, which could lead inadvertently into another disastrous war (this time with adversaries possessing nuclear weapons).

Therefore, in addition to concerns about the effects of fossil fuels on ecological degradation and wasteful public spending, people began to question the costs and risks of maintaining large militaries, whose purposes increasingly extended beyond self-defense to maintaining regional and global hegemonies for corrupt oligarchic regimes.

Considered together, these issues have generated a shift in world public opinion from acquiescence and acceptance toward outrage and activism. The sheer number, similarity and persistency of global demonstrations during 2020 are striking. Although some regard these protests as nihilistic mayhem, they have the hallmarks of a historic turning point: away from the neoclassical industrial paradigm toward the emerging life-mimicking one.

A new superpower in the making

As we reflect on these developments, the lessons of the Nordic Renaissance take on renewed significance. By approaching Nature and humanity as valuable partners rather than pawns in a quest for GDP and profit growth, we can discern a new way forward for people, planet and prosperity. To Otto Scharmer, such stirrings have aroused "a new superpower in the making" from all corners of the world. Similar to Bildung, this power resides in each of us as we self-develop and in the collective energy of our social awakenings.

To tap that energy, Scharmer and a small group of colleagues launched on March 27, 2020, a virtual organization called GAIA (Global Activation of Intention and Action) to mobilize "deep learning events for participants around the world." Noting the spontaneity of GAIA's creation, Scharmer observed: "All of this happened without much planning and on a dime – even without any real budget." Within 12 days of its birth, more than

10,000 people enrolled in a four-month collective learning journey offered by a core team of 100+ people on five language tracks.

> The remarkable response to GAIA is evidence, perhaps, of something much bigger. It signals the further awakening of a movement taking shape across the planet. It's the activation of a deep and widely held longing for profound societal and civilizational renewal.
>
> Otto Scharmer[14]

Although GAIA started in response to the coronavirus pandemic, it embraces a much larger agenda. As the failures of the neoclassical model become more and more evident, the number of GAIA supporters grew rapidly. The core issue underlying that growth is "a mindset of disconnect, competition and empire building" that is embedded in most governance systems rather than ones of interconnectivity and ecosystem awareness.

To redress this disconnect, GAIA has developed an "ecosystem of partners" based on seven core fundamentals (all of which are embedded in the Nordic Model). These include available "spaces" where individuals can pursue "deep learning" and understanding; processes for "strengthening the sources of health for people and planet"; localized "regenerative" food systems that collaborate with Nature; "mission-driven" corporate enterprises that serve rather than exploit life; responsible financial practices that provide resources for "evolving and transforming the system" and governance practices based on collective (egalitarian) "coordination."

Considered together, these seven fundamentals replicate the Nordic Model as described in this book by expanding our awareness (circles of belonging) "*both individually and collectively*" as responsible beings: aware of our impacts on each other and Nature through our spiritual affiliation with life. In doing so, the GAIA model declares we can change the trajectories of our lives. "No other species on earth can do this," Scharmer says. "It's what makes us human."

Will it work? It has certainly done so for the five Nordic countries. As other countries emulate the open democratic cultures of the Nordic world, they too have become more stable and sustainably prosperous as revealed in Chapter Five (Table 5.1).

An ecosystem of partners

The super power of economies that mimic life resides in their spirit of partnership. By seeing economies as they truly are, as sub-systems of life, not super-systems that transcend life, they generate extraordinary energy and operating leverage. This, as we have seen, is powerfully transformative.

By approaching the world from this perspective, Nordic countries organize as Nature does in cohesive, self-organizing (egalitarian) networks, which is why they are continually rated among the world's most progressive democracies. Their shared cultural DNA, embodied in a philosophy of education (Bildung), endows them with a capacity for systems thinking, which enables them to think beyond themselves (ego) to the health of the whole (eco) in which they exist. Their frugal instincts and behaviors impel them to conserve resources and use renewable energy (sun, wind, biomass, hydro) as Nature does. Their openness to feedback from each other and Nature – especially when negative feedback forces them to re-evaluate their behaviors – gives them a unique capacity for adaptive learning and green innovation. Their symbiotic sense of connection to the whole of life endows them with skills in co-operation and collaboration that extend their global reach and influence in world affairs. Also, their broad spectrum consciousness, their sense of being within the system, gives them strategic insight and prescience in long-term planning.

This life-mimicking system works brilliantly because life, broadly defined as people and Nature, is the primary source of all value. When countries recognize this essential fact and seek to partner with life (rather than exploit it), they release a wealth of operating leverage points.

With such plain facts, simple arguments and common sense, we have it in our power, as Thomas Paine said on the eve of the American Revolution, "to begin the world over again." By means of such clear reasoning, the Nordic Model has achieved a coherence and strength that offers humanity a viable way forward that the neoclassical model utterly lacks in its self-destructive quest for infinite GDP growth on our finite planet Earth.

Notes

1 Adam Smith. 1776. *The Wealth of Nations*. London: W. Strahan and T. Cadell Book 1, Chapter 8, p. 96.

2 Nordic Council of Ministers. 2019. "Our vision 2030." Adopted August 20. Available from: https://www.norden.org/en/declaration/our-vision-2030

3 Adam Smith. 1759. *The Theory of Moral Sentiments*. Edinburgh: Alexander Kincaid and J. Bell, p. 1.

4 Otto Sharmer. *Theory U*. Available from: http://www.ottoscharmer.com/sites/default/files/TU2_Intro_o.pdf

5 Otto Scharmer. "Coaching and consulting." Available from: https://www.ottoscharmer.com/consulting/leadership-development

6 Otto Scharmer. "Client and partner list." Available from: https://www.ottoscharmer.com/bio/client-list

7 Presencing Institute. "Innovation labs." Available from: https://www.presencing.org/labs/innovation-labs

8 Francesco de Pasquale. 2020. "Coronavirus: an anthropocene hybrid? The need for a geoethic perspective for the future of Earth," *AIMS Geosciences*. 6(1): pp. 131–4. Available from: https://www.aimspress.com/fileOther/PDF/geosciences/geosci-06-01-008.pdf

9 Otto Scarmer. 2020. "A new superpower in the making: awareness-based collective action." April 8. Available from: https://medium.com/presencing-institute-blog/a-new-superpower-in-the-making-awareness-based-collective-action-83861bcb9859

10 Borzou Daragahi. 2020. "Why the George Floyd protests went global," *The Atlantic Council*. June 10. Available from: https://www.atlanticcouncil.org/blogs/new-atlanticist/george-floyd-protests-world-racism/

11 David Coady et al. 2019. "Global fossil fuel subsidies remain large: an update based on country-level estimates," International Monetary Fund (IMF) Working Papers. May 2. Available from: https://www.imf.org/en/Publications/WP/Issues/2019/05/02/Global-Fossil-Fuel-Subsidies-Remain-Large-An-Update-Based-on-Country-Level-Estimates-46509

12 James Ellsmoor. 2019. "United States spends ten times more on fossil fuel subsidies than on education," *Forbes Magazine*. June 15. Available from: https://www.forbes.com/sites/jamesellsmoor/2019/06/15/united-states-spend-ten-times-more-on-fossil-fuel-subsidies-than-education/#2e8a9cbb4473

13 Javier Blas. 2019. "The biggest saudi oilfield is fading faster than anyone guessed," *Bloomberg*. April. Available from: https://www.bloomberg.com/news/articles/2019-04-02/saudi-aramco-reveals-sharp-output-drop-at-super-giant-oil-field

14 Op cit. Otto Scharmer. 2020. "A new superpower in the making: awareness-based collective action." April 8.

EPILOGUE

The Nordic region has the highest levels of social trust in the world, which benefits the economy, individuals and society as a whole.

Nordic Council of Ministers[1]

None are so hopelessly enslaved as those who falsely believe they are free.

Johan Wolfgang von Goethe

Economies are fundamentally sub-systems of life – not super-systems that are above and apart from life. Nordic countries recognize this essential truth, while those operating under the neoclassical/industrial model do not. That is why the life-mimicking Nordic Model has become the world's most effective and trusted approach to political-economic development. It is also why the small countries of Denmark, Finland, Sweden, Norway and Iceland are consistently rated among the world's freest and most prosperous nations while the once-thriving US is declining on both fronts.

Because of this crucial difference in cultural awareness and trust, Iceland today enjoys a higher living standard than the US. In spite of having a population of only 335,000, its government operates on balanced budgets while maintaining secure fully-funded universal safety nets. By contrast, the US runs up trillions of dollars in budget deficits and unfunded liabilities, which are now growing several times faster than gross domestic product (GDP).

Iceland's economic advantage can be seen in two critical metrics: its high labor participation rate (82%), which in 2019 was 19 percentage points higher than the US (63%)[2]; and its high per capita GDP ($67,037), which was 3% higher than the US ($65,112).[3] Beyond affording an elevated quality of life for Icelandic citizens, such productivity has enabled the country to develop a sovereign wealth fund at a time when the US economy is virtually drowning in debt.

In addition to these economic advantages, Iceland has one of the world's most robust democracies. According to the *Economist* Intelligence Unit's 2019 global democracy survey, it had the second-highest rating among 167 countries evaluated versus the US at twenty-fifth.[4] Congruent with this finding, Iceland was ranked sixth in the world in Delotte's 2019 Social Progress Index versus the US at twenty-sixth (Chapter Two) and fifth in the World Economic Forum's 2020 Social Mobility Index versus the US at twenty-seventh (Chapter Eight).

Further to these findings, Iceland was rated first in the world for the health of its citizens in a 2016 Lancet survey of world health conditions. By comparison, the US was rated twenty-eighth.[5] Reflecting this standard of care, the Icelandic government offered all citizens free coronavirus in the early months of the 2020 pandemic and tested a greater portion of its population for the virus than any other country. This enabled Iceland to achieve one of the world's highest recovery rates for those struck by the virus. The economic value of such respect and caring cannot be overstated. As shown throughout this book, the social trust it generates is evident in the desire of Nordic people to participate in the economy and give back to the communities that so thoughtfully support them.

Importance of culture

Biology determines what we need, and culture determines how we get it. When economies mimic life, they naturally place a high priority on nurturing people and Nature. We call this managing by means (MBM) because people and Nature are the primary means by which economies generate prosperity.

Beyond its logical appeal, MBM engages the spiritual (life-affirming) values of people, which are a crucial source of their creativity. Such values, as we have seen, are ingrained in the holistic Nordic approach to education, their openness to constructive feedback and their avid support for the UN's 2030 Sustainability Development Goals. They are also expressed in the region's entrepreneurial activity in renewable energy and circular economy innovation – activities that visibly give meaning and direction to the lives of Nordic citizens.

Neoclassical economists have difficulty understanding the power of such spiritual motivations because their mechanistic ways of thinking place a higher value on economic results, such as GDP and profit, than they do on life. Called management by results (MBR), this often justifies the exploitation of people and Nature – an order of priorities that has widened the gaps between rich and poor and set world economies on a self-destructive course of climate change, ecosystem degradation and species extinction. The cumulative effects of such adversities, including their harmful effects on human health and productivity, largely explain why living conditions in the once-prosperous US now lag those of Iceland.

Historically, it took a long time for this fundamental flaw in neoclassical political-economic theory to be widely recognized because economic advances during the 19th and 20th centuries appeared to outweigh such negative consequences. But from the mid-20th century onward, the tide began to turn as world population growth and expanding GDPs began to exceed Earth's biological carrying capacity.

Rather than taking a time out to consider the consequences of this turn of events, as Nordic countries did, the US (and other countries operating on neoclassical principles) decided to double down on MBR practices – oblivious to the fact that infinite growth on a finite planet is impossible. Therefore, instead of looking to the health of the whole in accordance with natural principles and the emerging field of systems theory, the US became more autocratic and self-preoccupied – conditions that sharply eroded the economic value of social trust in its governance system.

We find compelling evidence of this trend in the compensation gap between US corporate CEOs and those of their employees. According to *Forbes Magazine*, a US bi-weekly business journal, American CEOs in 2018 were paid 361 times the average compensation of their employees compared to just 20 times during the 1950s.[6] A more egregious example of such autocratic propensities occurred during the 2008/9 global financial crisis when Wall Street banks, which largely caused the crisis, awarded bonuses of more than $1 million each to about 5,000 bankers while their institutions were being bailed out at public expense.[7]

A further step toward oligarchy occurred in 2010 when the US Supreme Court reversed century-old campaign finance restrictions by ruling that corporations and lobbying groups could spend unlimited funds on elections. Known as the *Citizens United* decision, this contravened US democratic tradition by allowing political influence to be sold to the highest bidder. More than any prior decision, this solidified the power of fossil fuel companies, their bankers and allied industries, whose self-serving behaviors have accelerated the US economy's decline into unsustainable debt/GDP ratios, ecological degradation and social divisiveness. Given these facts, it is no wonder the US standard of living has fallen so far behind Iceland and the Nordic world.

Rays of hope

Although this adverse situation has become extreme in the US, which was once a progressive leader of the free world, it is not hopeless. So long as Americans and the citizens of other industrial democracies preserve their traditions of free elections, peaceful regime change and the rule of law, reform is possible. It will not be easy because elites at the center of political-economic power will resist mightily. But their leadership authority is waning, and people everywhere are pushing back harder against their abuses of power – a trend evident in the extraordinary worldwide burst of public demonstrations following the murder by US police of an unarmed black man in 2020.[8]

In the midst of this breakdown of the neoclassical model of political-economy, the life-mimicking Nordic Model offers a plausible way forward. By preserving the best elements of democracy and free market enterprise, it has become the world's most effective form of governance. Whether we call it the Nordic Model or refer to it by some other name, it is the only foreseeable way the world can escape the system's trap of neoclassical political-economic management.

In the meantime, those of us who can see the big picture must use our knowledge and will to uphold the finest elements of our cultures while discarding the destructive and unethical parts we are now struggling to escape. The once alluring vision that the neoclassical/industrial model would set us free toward a new era of unbounded prosperity has collapsed under the weight of its inherent contradictions. As we awaken to this reality, we are reminded of Goethe's insightful remark that "None are so hopelessly enslaved as those who falsely believe they are free."

True freedom, in fact, resides in joining the natural flow of life rather than trying to control or conquer it. As Donella Meadows put it in her brilliant essay, "Dancing with Systems," we cannot control living systems or figure them out because they are always changing. We can, however, "listen to what the system tells us, and discover how its properties and our values can work together to bring forth something much better than could ever be produced by our will alone."[9]

That is why the life-mimicking model works. It does not mean we will not fail in what we do. But if we listen to what social and biospheric systems tell us, we can learn from our mistakes and move ahead into a world of sustainable prosperity.

Notes

1 Nordic Council of Ministers. 2017. "Trust – The nordic gold." Cover page. Available from: https://norden.diva-portal.org/smash/get/diva2:1095959/FULLTEXT02.pdf

2 Trading Economics. "Labor force participation rates 2019." Available from: https://tradingeconomics.com/country-list/labor-force-participation-rate

3 Statistics Times. "Projected GDP per capita ranking 2019." Available from: http://statisticstimes.com/economy/projected-world-gdp-capita-ranking.php

4 The Economist Intelligence Unit. "The world's most democratic countries by rank." The Democracy Index 2019. Available from: https://www.eiu.com/topic/democracy-index?&zid=democracyindex2019&utm_source=blog&utm_medium=blog&utm_name=democracyindex2019&utm_term=democracyindex2019&utm_content=middle_link

5 The Lancet. 2016. "Measuring the health-related sustainable development goals of 188 countries: a baseline analysis from the globla burden of didease Study 2015," *The Lancet.* 388(10053): pp.1813–50, October 8, 2016. Available

from: https://www.thelancet.com/journals/lancet/issue/vol388no10053/PII S0140-6736(16)X0042-6

6 Diana Hembree. 2018. "CEO pay skyrockets to 361 times that of the average worker," *Forbes Magazine*. May 22. Available from: https://www.forbes.com/sites/dianahembree/2018/05/22/ceo-pay-skyrockets-to-361-times-that-of-the-average-worker/#6d4d4a72776d

7 Louise Story and Eric Dash. 2009. "Bankers reaped lavish bonuses during bailouts," *New York Times*. July 30. Available from: https://www.nytimes.com/2009/07/31/business/31pay.html

8 Wikipedia. "List of George Floyd protests outside the United States." June 2020. Available from: https://en.wikipedia.org/wiki/List_of_George_Floyd_protests_outside_the_United_States

9 Donella Meadows. 2001. "Dancing with systems," Available from: http://donellameadows.org/archives/dancing-with-systems/

APPENDIX ONE

LEVERAGE POINTS IN ECONOMIC DEVELOPMENT

Leverage points are places in a complex system (an economy, an ecosystem, a living body), where a small shift in one thing can produce big changes in everything. To illustrate how such leverage works, systems thinker Donella Meadows used the metaphor of an iceberg. This symbolically draws our attention to the reality that the 10% we see above the water (economic results) is in fact supported by a much larger mass of thoughtful activity below the surface. As shown in Figure A.1, this large below-water metaphoric mass consists of the *beliefs* (mental models, assumptions) we use in defining our economies; the *visions and values* we hold as we forge paths to the future; the organizational *structures* that emerge from these aspirations (which determine how effectively information flows) and the life-mimicking *behaviors* that ultimately determine economic results.

As indicated by the arrow on the right side of the diagram, the deeper we go toward life-affirming beliefs, visions and values, the more leverage we attain in achieving sustainable economic development. Leverage is greatest when people understand the value of living and working in harmony with Nature. In Nordic countries, such eco-centric thinking is embedded in their respectful democratic traditions and holistic philosophy of education – virtues that can be learned anywhere.

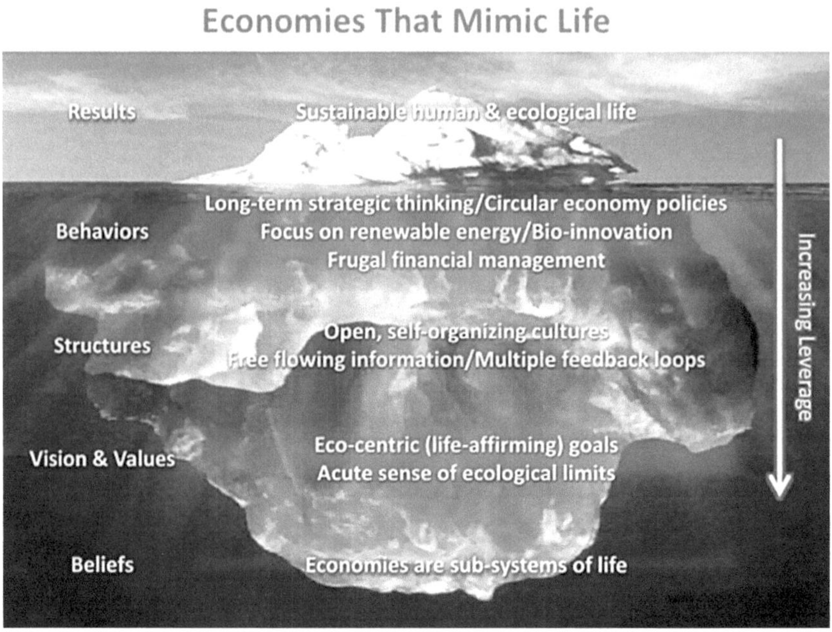

Figure A.1 Economic Leverage Points

Paradigms as the sources of systems

The paradigm in this diagram is the belief that economies are sub-systems of life. From this ideal, everything naturally flows as we rise to the top of the iceberg. In sum, when our mental models and governance practices shift from the ego-centric paradigm that our economies are super-systems that transcend life to the eco-centric paradigm that our economies are sub-systems of life, we create new, more robust pathways to the future. In doing so, we implicitly recognize that people and Nature are the sources (means) of all value creation.

Because of this, as we look to the future, our visions and values naturally embrace goals that respect ecological limits and reinforce life. Economies that hold such goals, as shown throughout this book, generate an abundance of valuable resources compared to those that exploit life in their pursuit of gross domestic product (GDP). To achieve such results, they organize in ways that facilitate open exchanges of information and systemic feedback – qualities that enable them to discern the health and wellbeing of people and Nature, which are the primary sources of their prosperity.

These organizational (structural) qualities inform long-term strategic planning and circular (life-mimicking) innovations, which themselves are
sources of leverage.

Considered as such, when economies operate as sub-systems of life, they
benefit from a cascade of leverage points. The measurable results we get
from this are technologies that continually refresh the resources we need
to survive and thrive. Among these, renewable energy, bio-innovation and
circular economy practices support a sustainable prosperity that requires
little debt to maintain. Compared to the older industrial model of capitalism, which is drowning in its carbon emissions, waste and debt, it is the
clear, pragmatic way forward.

APPENDIX TWO

NORDIC COMPANIES IN THE GLOBAL 100

The following 37 Nordic corporations have been named by Corporate Knights on their annual lists of the world's 100 most sustainable companies. Twenty-seven of these have been listed multiple times and nineteen (printed in bold type) have been listed in the top twenty-five one or more times. For the year 2020, Nordic companies took the top three rankings (Ørsted, Hansen and Neste). This is a remarkable record for a region with a population of only 26 million (less than half of 1% of the world's population). Such data affirms the operating leverage of economies that mimic life as shown in Appendix One.

Table A.1 Nordic Companies in the Global 100

Company	2020	2019	2018	2017	2016	2015	2014	2013	2012	2011
AAK AB		*								
Atlas Copco					*	*	*	*	*	
Coloplast								*	*	
Danske Bank				*	*	*			*	
DNB				*	*	*		*		
Electrolux		*							*	
Ericcson	*									
Chr. Hansen	*	*	*							
Hennes & Mauritz	*		*	*	*	*	*	*	*	*
Holmen				*						
Husqvarna							*			
Kesco	*	*	*	*	*	*		*		
Kone	*	*				*				
Metso	*	*								
Neste	*	*	*	*		*	*	*	*	*
Nokia		*		*	*	*	*			*
Nordea Bank		*	*							
Norsk Hydro									*	*
Novo Nordisk	*	*			*	*	*	*	*	*
Novozymes	*			*		*		*	*	*
Orkla			*							
Ørsted	*	*	*							
Outotec	*	*	*	*	*	*	*	*		
Kesco				*			*		*	*
Sandvik			*							
Scania							*	*	*	
SEB (Bank)	*				*	*	*			
Svenska Cellulosa		*								
Statoil/Equinor				*	*	*	*		*	*
Stora Enso										*
Storebrand	*		*	*	*	*	*	*	*	*
Telenor				*	*			*		
Teliasonera									*	
Tomra Systems									*	
UPM Kymenne	*	*		*						
Vestas Wind	*	*	*						*	*
Wartsila			*							

APPENDIX THREE

NORDIC ECOLOGICAL FOOTPRINT

Although Nordic countries are world leaders in renewable energy production and circular economy innovation, their per capita ecological footprints are three to four times higher than the world's average per capita biocapacity as defined by the Global Footprint Network (GFN).

The ecological footprint is an accounting metric that assesses the resource *demand* humanity puts on Nature relative to the *supply* of bioproductive land and water measured in terms of global hectares (gha).[1] According to the GFN's 2019 analysis, which is based on 2016 data, the world-average ecological footprint at that time was 2.75 gha/person. Compared to the world-average biocapacity of 1.63 gha/person, that means the world economy was then running an ecological deficit of 1.12 gha – resulting in a 68.7% overshoot.[2] GFN estimates based on incomplete data suggest a 2019 global overshoot in the vicinity of 75 percent.

As shown in Table A.2, the per capita ecological footprints of Nordic countries range from a low of 5.6 (Norway) to a high of 6.9 (Denmark). While all but Denmark live within their biocapacity reserves, due to the region's low population density and vast forest resources, Nordic countries remain far from their goals of living and working within the world's ecological budget. Nevertheless, over the past 50 years, Nordic countries have made significant reductions in their ecological footprints while at the same time increasing their standards of living.

Because a large portion of the Nordic region's ecological footprint is due to the sourcing of imported goods, Nordic companies place high priorities on greening their global supply chains. In doing so, they actively support the

Table A.2 Nordic ecological footprints relative to biocapacity: in terms of gha/
person with a summary of 50-year footprint results[3]

Country	Per Capita Biocapacity	Per Capita Footprint	Biocapacity Reserve/Deficit	50-year Footprint Trend		
				High	Low	Reduction
Denmark	4.2	6.8	−2.6	9.4	6.8	28%
Finland	12.6	6.3	6.3	7.8	6.3	19%
Norway	7.3	5.5	1.8	11.2	5.5	51%
Sweden	12.1	6.3	3.4	8.5	6.4	25%

UN's sustainable development goals (SDGs) – often in partnership with the
Nordic Council of Ministers.[4] Their success in doing so is affirmed by the
extraordinary number of Nordic companies named to the Global 100 of
sustainability leaders over the past decade, as shown in Appendix Two.

In addition, a new generation of entrepreneurs is emerging who are per-
sonally committed to global footprint mitigation. As mentioned in Chapter
Two, their initiatives include the Nordic Cleantech Open and Helsinki's
annual student-led Slush gathering, whose Global Impact Accelerator (GIA)
supports sustainability entrepreneurs in the emerging markets of Africa,
Asia and Latin America.[5] Funded by Finland's Ministry of Foreign Affairs,
the GIA partners with organizations worldwide to find candidate startups,
provide them with training and give them a chance to gain exposure at the
world's biggest annual startup event in Helsinki. During its first three years
(2017–19) GIA launched more than 70 startups.[6] While that is not enough
in itself to turn the tide on greening world supply chains, it indicates an
important move in that direction by young Nordic entrepreneurs.

Notes

1 Ecological Footprint. Our Work. https://www.footprintnetwork.org/our-wor
k/ecological-footprint/
2 Global Footprint Network. York University. Footprint Data Foundation
(FODAF).   https://data.footprintnetwork.org/#/countryTrends?cn=5001
&type=BCpc,EFCpc
3 Ibid. Reference 2016 on website chart. https://data.footprintnetwork.org/#/
(Data year 2016)
4 The Nordic Council of Ministers. Vision for 2030. https://www.norden.org/
en/information/generation-2030-nordic-programme-agenda-2030
5 PwC Sri Lanka. "SLUSH global impact accelerator." Available from: https://
www.pwc.com/lk/en/what-is-slush-global-impact-accelerator.html
6 News.slush.org. June 2018. "GIA success stories - where are they now?"
Available from: https://news.slush.org/news/towards-sustainable-develop
ment-goals-meet-slush-global-impact-accelerator-startups/

APPENDIX FOUR

THE FALLACY OF DEBT LEVERAGE

To neoclassical economists, debt is an effective form of operating leverage because it can multiply economic activity during episodes of slow growth. While this works when debt levels are low and economic capacity is underutilized, continuous borrowing can become a downward spiral when the cost of debt service exceeds an economy's income generating capacity over an extended period of time. For this reason, debt is a limited tool at best.

The following chart from the US Federal Reserve Economic Data (FRED) repository in St. Louis shows how the growth of aggregate US debt (all sectors) began to outrun gross domestic product (GDP) in the early 1970s – the same time the world's ecological footprint began to exceed Earth's biological carrying capacity as shown in Appendix Three.[1] While correlation is not causation, both events are symptoms of economic overreach and a shared hubristic belief among neoclassical economists that infinite growth on a finite planet is feasible and in humanity's best interests.

The US has made this problem worse by under-funding promised health care and retirement benefits: an implicit form of debt called "unfunded liabilities." To understand the scope of this problem, the federal government spends roughly 60% of its budget on such "entitlements." However, the public trust funds it created to help with this funding have been rapidly depleting.

As shown Figure A.X, the trust funds for Disability Insurance (DI) and Old Age Security Insurance (OASI), which are funded by employee payroll

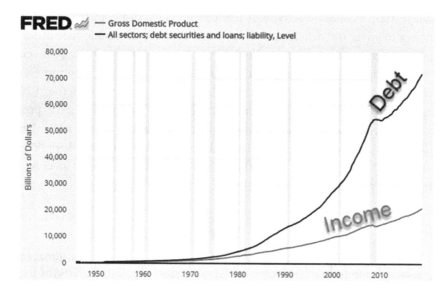

Figure A.2

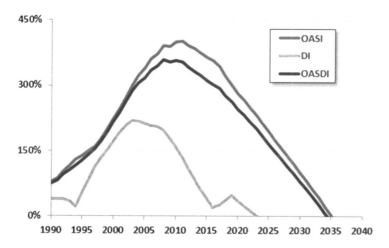

Figure A.3 Social security trust fund asset ratio (percent of annual benefit). (Source: Social Security Administration.)

deductions, are expected to run down by 2024 and 2035, respectively. Employee funded trusts for Medicare and Medicaid are in similar straits. Consequently, the only sustainable way the federal government can continue these programs is to raise taxes and/or cut benefits – both of which will restrain economic activity. A less proven way is to continue printing money to cover the deficits, a strategy that misprices economic risk, misallocates resources and devalues the dollar in terms of its purchasing power.

In addition to US government arrearages, state and local governments have substantial debts and unfunded liabilities of their own. With the 2020 coronavirus pandemic adding trillions more to these burdens, the presumed leverage of debt has become a black hole leaving the US and other excessively debt-leveraged countries with fewer and fewer strategic options compared to the Nordics and other countries that have lower sovereign debt ratios and no unfunded liabilities.

Note

1 FRED database. Chart of US debt vs. GDP since 1950. https://images. search.yahoo.com/yhs/search   p=fred+us+debt+vs+gdp+chart&fr=yhs-trp-001&hspart=trp&hsimp=yhs-001&imgurl=http%3A%2F%2Fwww.economic-undertow.com%2Fwp-content%2Fuploads%2F2015%2F06%2FF red-GDP-debt-061515-1024x639.png#id=0&iurl=http%3A%2F%2Fwww. economic-undertow.com%2Fwp-content%2Fuploads%2F2015%2F06%2FF red-GDP-debt-061515-1024x639.png&action=click

INDEX

Page numbers in "italic" indicate a figure and page numbers in "bold" indicate a table.

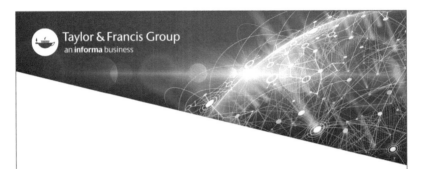

Taylor & Francis eBooks

www.taylorfrancis.com

A single destination for eBooks from Taylor & Francis
with increased functionality and an improved user
experience to meet the needs of our customers.

90,000+ eBooks of award-winning academic content in
Humanities, Social Science, Science, Technology, Engineering,
and Medical written by a global network of editors and authors.

TAYLOR & FRANCIS EBOOKS OFFERS:

A streamlined
experience for
our library
customers

A single point
of discovery
for all of our
eBook content

Improved
search and
discovery of
content at both
book and
chapter level

REQUEST A FREE TRIAL
support@taylorfrancis.com

Routledge
Taylor & Francis Group

CRC Press
Taylor & Francis Group